PANAVIA
TORNADO

Above: First take-off of 03, the first dual-pilot version, showing forward facing camera near top of fin; later this was replaced by regular ARI.18228 aerial, and a flight-refuelling probe was added on the right side. Blow-in inlet doors can be seen fully open under the wing glove./*BAe*

PANAVIA
Modern Combat Aircraft 6
TORNADO

Bill Gunston

LONDON

IAN ALLAN LTD

Above: Prototype 03 with four Kormorans and two Ajax, with No 2 engine in afterburner. Among many other features are a row of nine vortex generators on the fin, added in 1977; the production aircraft have five only./*BAe*

First published 1980

ISBN 0 71101009 9

Published by Ian Allan Ltd, Shepperton, Surrey, and printed
by Ian Allan Printing Ltd at their works at
Coombelands in Runnymede, England.

Contents

Left: Beautiful portrait of the last pre-production aircraft, 16, in MFG livery and with four Kormorans; this is the kind of 200ft/90m environment in which Tornados will live./*Panavia*

Preface

Unlike the other books in this series, this volume deals with a very new aeroplane only just entering service. But it has still been around long enough to be judged not merely of exceptional merit but almost certainly the most useful single type of military aircraft in the world today. And that is only one facet to a story rich in technical boffinry, human relations and the just triumph of patient engineers over many difficulties.

Some of the difficulties were concerned with the unique demands made of this aeroplane, which had to do everything and yet meet severe limitations on physical size and price. More difficult was the basic task of political survival. Tornado, originally known as MRCA (for Multi-Role Combat Aircraft), was conceived by three strongly different countries in Europe, each with great pride in its own capabilities. In these countries three air forces and a navy each spelt out their own set of demands. Then a team of engineers from the three nations set about meeting those demands. Any one set of requirements would have been a challenge; four might have been met by four different aircraft, but the idea was to meet them with one. Nothing like it had been done before.

On top of these valid problems were a host of unnecessary difficulties caused by the political environment. In Britain the government had lately cancelled all the new crop of home-grown combat aircraft and replaced them with American purchases, saying that the aircraft industry had 'failed the nation' and feeding the public a stream of astronomic costs, or supposed savings (by buying foreign aircraft), to create the impression that building one's own combat aircraft was done only by lunatics. Both in Britain and in Italy a substantial proportion of the Members of Parliament sincerely believed that defence was undesirable, and that money spent on it should be transferred to more socially desirable objectives. In FRG (Federal Republic of Germany) there were strong political and financial pressures to purchase equipment from the United States, to pay for the US forces in Central Europe.

Meanwhile, the media in most countries inside and outside NATO had gradually – and not unreasonably – come to regard major aircraft programmes in a totally different light, depending on the country of origin. If it was American or French it was taken for granted even at the paper stage, and even today potential customers go so far as to 'short-list' such aircraft before they have been developed and long before any figure for the price can bear any meaningful relationship to what the customer might eventually have to pay. But if the aircraft is British the media's chief preoccupation has been the date of cancellation. When the aircraft appears to be technically advanced, as in the case of MRCA, the obvious way to create a 'story' is to present the whole project as desperately complicated and expensive, and, if possible, as either useless or else inferior to some real or imagined wonder-plane from America or France. This appears to be thought the only way to attract the attention of the public, and in the case of Tornado it has been done in at least four major TV programmes, 10 radio feature broadcasts and 270 newspaper articles in Britain alone.

Perhaps the media are right. Maybe shrill attacks on the most important weapon programme in Western Europe and one of the greatest international collaborative projects in all history have indeed interested the public. But most people are not entirely

disinterested in a story of success; and the true story of Tornado is one of success, against very long odds, that is wholly exceptional in its completeness. The last book I wrote in this series dealt with an American aircraft designed to fly generally similar missions, the F-111. Though this was created by large teams of skilful and dedicated engineers in the richest country in the world, nothing seemed to go right (and it was a one-country programme). The contrast with Tornado could hardly be more vivid.

It is also worth noting that if war were ever to come in Western Europe, it would do so at night, in fog, rain or snow. No tactical aircraft in NATO could fly, except a handful of F-111s. Thanks to Tornado, the number of aircraft able to take off will grow by 809.

Thousands of engineers, officials, and specialists in uniforms of various colours, have created Tornado in the past ten years. Most of them have been at it so hard they never had time to stand back and look at what they were doing. Then, in 1978, they began to be visited by possible customers from outside the three nations. In making their presentations to these visitors they were able to see that they had built something unique. Their achievement is so great that it cannot suddenly be rivalled by a competitor or adversary. Much of the credit is due to a handful of men of true greatness who had the vision and force of character to take correct decisions in many situations where these decisions might have seemed to be acts of weakness or even surrender. For example, Italy makes the wings which are pivoted to the German centre fuselage, but the flexible fairings over the slot into which each wing folds are a British responsibility. Think how tempting it is for each partner, in ten thousand localised design or development problems, to achieve a solution at the expense of the other! It is almost instinctive for big companies to exploit the weakness of others; Tornado was achieved by doing just the opposite and building on one's partners' strengths.

Tornado is now in full production. Because of it, Western Europe is less likely to be attacked. Because of it, Western Europe is not dependent on the United States for its combat aircraft. And perhaps the greatest importance of this programme to history is the sheer magnitude of the international collaboration which it demonstrates. If we go on like this we may eventually wonder just what we mean by the word 'foreign'.

Bill Gunston
Haslemere 1979

Below: MBB flight-test crew in front of 07 at the Hanover air show in April 1978; they came to watch the show, not because a Tornado needs looking after to this extent./*MBB*

Below: Beautiful portrait of 06 pulling round in a tight turn; there is condensation vapour above the wings, and in the original the slightly sooty trail from the engines can be seen at an angle contrasting with the tip vortices. Note undernose fairing and gear in navigator's cockpit./*BAe*

Glossary

A&AEE   Aeroplane & Armament Experimental Establishment.
ADF   Automatic direction finding.
ADV   Air-defence version.
AEW   Airborne early-warning.
AGE   Aerospace ground equipment.
AMI   Aeronautica Militare Italiano (Italian air force).
AMRAAM   Advanced medium-range air-to-air missile.
APU   Auxiliary power unit.
ATAF   Allied Tactical Air Force.
ATS   Automatic test station.
avionics   Aviation electronics.
az/el   Azimuth and elevation.
BAC   British Aircraft Corporation (now part of BAe).
BAe   British Aerospace.
BITE   Built-in test equipment.
CAP   Combat air patrol.
CAS   Chief of the Air Staff.
CDMT   Central design and management team.
CoS   Chief of Staff.
CSAS   Command/stability augmentation system.
CSDE   Central Servicing Development Establishment (RAF).
DCoS   Deputy Chief of Staff.
DDOR   Deputy Director of Operational Requirements.
DINS   Digital inertial navigation system.
DOR   Director of Operational Requirements.
EBW   Electron-beam welding.
ECCM   Electronic counter-countermeasures.
ECM   Electronic countermeasures.
EW   Electronic warfare.
EWR   Entwicklungsring Süd.
FR   Flight refuelling.
FRG   Federal Republic of Germany.
GAF   Luftwaffe.
GNF   Marineflieger.
glove   Fixed inner section of wing.
HDD   Head-down display, in cockpit.

HUD   Head-up display, on glass screen focussed at infinity so as not to impair pilot's forward vision.
hydrazine   Monofuel $N_2 H_4$
I-band   Radar frequencies 8 to 10 GHz.
IDS   Interdiction/strike.
IFF   Identification friend or foe.
Imp gal   Imperial gallon, 1.2 US gallons.
INS   Inertial navigation system.
IR   Infra-red (heat).
J-band   Radar frequencies 10 to 20 GHz.
JaboG   Jagdbombengeschwader, fighter/bomber wing.
JIC   Joint Industrial Company.
Krüger   Hinged flap under inboard leading edge or glove.
Lance   Line algorithm for navigation in a combat environment.
lox   Liquid oxygen.
LRU   Line-replaceable unit.
MBB   Messerschmitt-Bölkow-Blohm.
MEPU   Monofuel emergency power unit.
MEZ   Missile engagement zone.
MFG   Marinefliegergeschwader, naval air wing.
Mintech   Ministry of Technology (UK, defunct).
MRCA   Multi-role combat aircraft.
MSDS   Marconi Space & Defence Systems.
MTU   Motoren-und-Turbinen Union.
NAMMA   NATO MRCA Management Agency.
NAMMO   NATO MRCA Management Organization.
OTC   Official test centre.
PRF   Pulse repetition frequency.
RHAW   Radar homing and warning.
R&D   Research and development.
RWR   Rear-warning radar.
SAM   Surface-to-air missile.
SDR   System design responsibility.
SEP   Specific excess power, surplus engine thrust available for climb or manoeuvre.
spoiler   Surface hinged above wing serving as primary roll control or secondary lift-dumper.
swing-wing   Having outer (main) wing sections pivoted, also called variable-sweep or VG.
TFR   Terrain-following radar.
three-spool   Engine having three concentric rotating assemblies.
TI   Texas Instruments Inc.
TTTE   Tri-national Tornado Training Establishment.
TWT   Travelling-wave tube.
uhf   Ultra-high frequency.
UKADGE   United Kingdom air-defence ground environment.
VAS   Visual augmentation system.
VCoS   Vice-Chief of Staff.
VG   Variable-geometry.
WP   Warsaw Pact.

Roots

On 5 July 1967 Denis Healey, who was then the British Minister of Defence, rose to his feet in the House of Commons and announced that France had withdrawn from the Anglo-French Variable-Geometry aircraft project. Previously he had himself described AFVG as 'militarily and industrially the core of our long-term aircraft programme', and when someone reminded him of this he quipped that he had looked up the meaning of 'core' in a dictionary and found it to be 'the central part, normally to be cut out'.

Almost unnoticed amidst the jeers and shouts was his news that he was authorising the British companies involved – at that time BAC (British Aircraft Corporation) on the airframe and Bristol Siddeley on the

engine – to continue variable-geometry project studies to an amended specification. This was by no means to be expected. Britain's government had spent 10 years denying any need for manned combat aircraft, three years fulminating against the anti-social planemakers, and was negotiating to buy 50 of the large and costly American F-111K variable-geometry bombers for the RAF.

BAC had, in fact, been one of the original pioneers of variable-geometry 'swing wings'. Sir Barnes Wallis at Weybridge had done more work on the idea in the decade following World War II than anyone else, and later his colleagues at Warton, Lancashire, discovered how great are the potential gains of a wing that can be spread out to a wide span, festooned with high-lift slats and flaps, for STOL (short take-off and landing) with heavy loads, cleaned up and pivoted slightly back for

Right: General-arrangement of the definitive AFVG, showing TSR.2-type inlets, inboard pivots leaving a gap between gloves and swept leading edges, and location of the three external loads. Length would have been 57ft 2.5in, compared with 54ft 9in for IDS Tornado which carries several times the weapon load./*BAC*

Below: Two-view drawings of the six main BAC projects from the P.45 via AFVG (next three) and UKVG to the point at which MRCA talks began in 1968./*BAe and Royal Aeronautical Society*

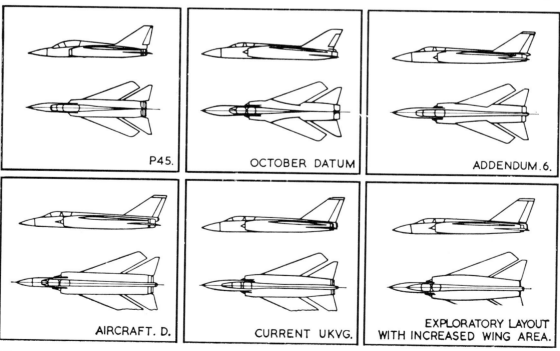

P45.

OCTOBER DATUM

ADDENDUM.6.

AIRCRAFT. D.

CURRENT UKVG.

EXPLORATORY LAYOUT WITH INCREASED WING AREA.

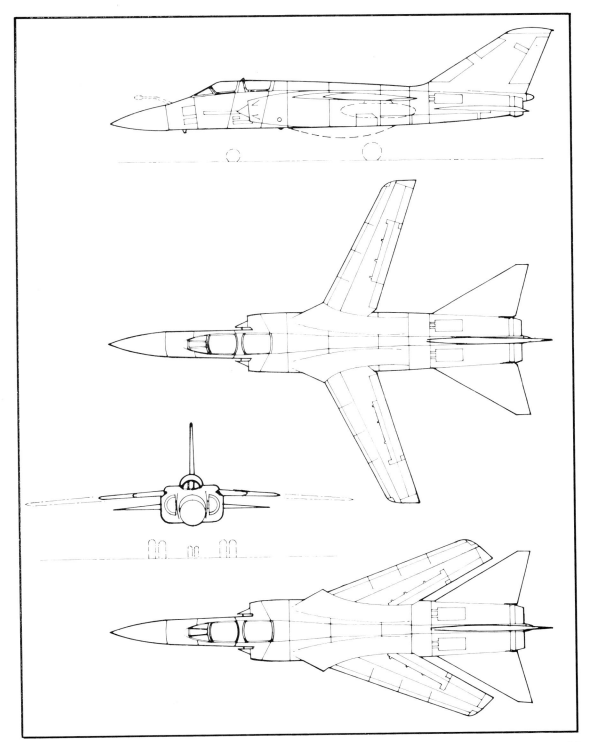

11

efficient subsonic cruise, swept to a greater angle for maximum power of manoeuvre in air combat, and finally folded right back for smooth supersonic flight through gusts and turbulence at tree-top height. The more missions a combat aircraft has to fly, the more it needs a swing-wing; but pioneering such a major advance without government interest was difficult. In 1958 the Warton team, working on a specification called GOR.339, which led ultimately to TSR.2, studied variable sweep as a possible solution. Test rigs were built at both Warton and at the Weybridge factory of Vickers, but when the two companies merged to form the nucleus of BAC in order to build TSR.2 they agreed there were too many unknowns

Above: When the first murmurings of what became Tornado reached the British Press, newspapers said it should be abandoned in favour of trying to join the US/German AVS (Advanced Vertical Strike) project. This incredibly complicated V/STOL machine would have pleased Rolls-Royce, who would have had six engines on each one. Fortunately for NATO it ground to a halt./*Rolls-Royce*

and risks and, regretfully, designed TSR.2 with a fixed wing.

Nevertheless the Warton team drew a family of projects called P.45 with variable sweep of a neater type, with the wing roots not sliding but pivoted at a fixed point, and this eventually formed a starting point for

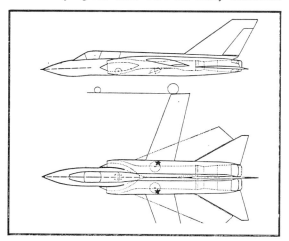

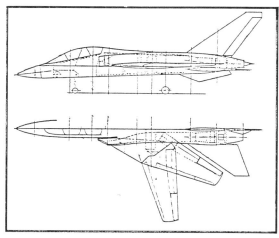

the AFVG. When the latter was abandoned the studies continued under such names as UKVG, VGCA, ACA (Advanced Combat Aircraft) and FCA (F for Future). Though outwardly nothing much seemed to be happening, the year from July 1967 was valuable in that, with unswerving support from Dr. W. Stewart at the Ministry of Technology (he had been Director of Anglo-French Trainer and VG projects and continued to shoulder responsibility for the subsequent studies), the BAC engineers were able to do enough testing to perfect two areas that were vital to building a VG aeroplane. One was the wing pivot bearing and the highly stressed wing roots and centre-section box linking the pivots, all of which gave major trouble on the F-111. The other was the high-lift slats and flaps which were essential if the full gains of VG were to be realised.

By mid-1968 BAC Warton had built and tested an excellent wing pivot using a Teflon bearing, which demonstrated the required safe life for fatigue-free service in the most demanding of all kinds of flying: low-level transonic attack. Another and more comprehensive full-scale rig proved the centre wing box, not as a research tool but as a proposed production item built by hard tooling and subjected to production-type inspection. Rolls-Royce, which in 1966 had taken over Bristol Siddeley, worked with the Warton team to establish the ideal by-pass ratio and thermodynamic cycle of the engine. There were dozens of existing or paper engines, but it was soon established that all fell short of the ideal by significant margins. The Derby company's new technology of high-pressure three-shaft engines proved ideally suited to the conflicting demands of a multi-role aircraft and to promise an excellent match with an advanced afterburner; but a new engine would be very costly. This sharply increased the pressure for a multinational collaborative project.

Even before the AFVG dust had settled, on 10 July 1967, a team from Warton visited Munich. A new building in that city housed the headquarters of EWR-Sud, an aircraft-industry consortium formed in 1959 by Heinkel, Messerschmitt and Bölkow to develop a Mach 2 V/STOL aircraft to a NATO requirement. EWR had later become a subsidiary of the new giant Messerschmitt-Bölkow-Blohm (MBB), and in place of

Far left: The BAC proposal for MRCA, late December 1968, with wing above the inlet ducts and thus a horizontal tail high enough for drop-out engines./*BAe*

Left: In contrast, the MBB proposal of late December 1968 had a mid-mounted wing, and thus a low tailplane and pull-out engines; but it did have fixed wing gloves and the important outboard pivots. / *MBB*

the original project was collaborating with the United States on an even more ambitious and complex AVS (Advanced Vertical Strike) aircraft. MBB was teamed with Fairchild Republic on this supersonic single-seater which featured swing-out lift engines in the forward fuselage. While British newspapers urged Whitehall to abandon support for British aircraft designs and instead join up with AVS, the truth of the matter was that AVS was in deep technical, political and financial trouble, and Washington was expected to pull out at the end of the definition phase in October 1967.

Quite apart from these problems, the whole philosophy of NATO war scenarios was at this time being turned upside-down. The aircraft projects of the early 1960s, including AVS, were based on the 'Massive Retaliation' doctrine, in which the slightest aggression against Western Europe was to be countered by nuclear war, which meant V/STOL and small bomb loads. By 1967 the 'Flexible Response' formula, despite its obvious drawbacks to an under-armed West, had been accepted instead. This had many effects on weapon planning, self-evident ones for aircraft being a great increase in payload delivered with a much greater degree of precision.

BAC proposed collaboration with UKVG or other P.45-derived swing-wing aircraft, with immediate adoption of Jaguar (to be made partly in Germany) as an interim aircraft. This sensible proposal was eventually not accepted, partly because of the effective presentations made by engineers from Northrop who convinced the Luftwaffe that it would be possible to design a single multi-mission aircraft much simpler and lighter than AVS. This torpedoed a Jaguar/ UKVG deal, but it also helped kill AVS. In the second half of 1967 the MBB engineers increasingly stopped working on AVS and got down to non-jet-lift studies of an NKF (Neuen Kampfflugzeug) not especially different from Warton's studies. Engineers and diplomats from Munich and Bonn talked to all possible collaborators, but BAC seemed by far the best bet because of common objectives and timescale.

In fact MBB's engineers at Munich appeared at times to be working on NKF with some reluctance, though accepting it as a political necessity. They welcomed the various ruses adopted by the officials to try to get formal collaboration started. (A typical ruse was an unpaid, no-strings study by BAC for the Luftwaffe on how many engines its future combat aircraft should have.) Since 13 July 1967 official meetings to explore collaboration had been in progress in London, Bonn and Rome, and by May 1968 the three countries involved had been joined by the Netherlands, Belgium and Canada. Britain's UKVG had become ACA (Advanced Combat Aircraft) and had then become a national submission to the multinational MRA-75, Multi-Role Aircraft for 1975. A central factor in making a collaborative aircraft possible was Britain's abandonment of 'east-of-Suez' commitments, which allowed radius of action to be scaled down to a purely European deployment matching the studies of other nations.

There were valuable inputs by all participants, Canada feeding in various contemporary American data and, with the Dutch, demanding extremely high SEP (Specific Excess Power, a measure of the surplus engine thrust available for climb or manoeuvre) and great combat manoeuvrability. Britain never wavered from the RAF's central demand that the aircraft should have two seats and a wholly exceptional kit of all-weather navigation and weapon-delivery systems. The Luftwaffe had a fixation on STOL performance (rightly, in the author's opinion) and insisted on being able to operate with its runways cratered and unusable. A political factor which at times clouded the issue was that, in addition to being rightly concerned to pick the right aircraft with which to replace its 970 F-104G Starfighters, the Germans insisted that, as they were going to buy 'far more than any other country', they should have design leadership of any eventual multinational programme.

This book is not the place to define the different kinds of tactical air mission, and in any case despite NATO's wish for standardisation there are differences between one air force's interpretations and another. The important factor in this context is that all the participating forces were thinking in terms not of 'a fighter' or 'a bomber' but of a multi-role aircraft for conventional warfare. But no two countries had exactly the same idea of what was wanted, or of how the various conflicting design factors (discussed in the next chapter) should be balanced. Canada and the Netherlands were insistent that the primary mission should be air superiority, the traditional 'fighter' mission, calling for long loiter time, high flight performance, unsurpassed manoeuvrability and, of course, radar and weapons configured for air-to-air use. Interdiction/strike (IDS) — the dominant requirement of the RAF — and naval strike demand all-weather navigation at tree-top height, large weapon payload and automated air/ground delivery (aiming) systems. Interdiction/close air support calls for operation from rough forward airstrips with heavy weapon load, good protection against ground fire and many features to enhance survivability, as well as the best in weapon delivery systems. Aircraft able to fly these missions ought to have no difficulty in meeting the demands of reconnaissance and, with dual flight controls, training. However, there is another mission demanding quite different radar and weapons, the air defence/interception (ADI) mission; this again calls for exceptional range and endurance, and, because long

runways should be available, can be flown by an aircraft heavier than the others, not because of weapons but because of large fuel capacity.

In July 1968 the governments of Britain, Federal Germany, Italy, Canada, the Netherlands and Belgium signed a Memorandum of Understanding expressing joint interest in an MRA-75 and a desire to conduct joint studies. By this time the national air staffs had prepared a vast all-embracing OEO (Operational Equipment Objective) which laid down every possible national demand: runway length and strength, weapon load, time to height, loiter endurance, mission radius at different heights, SEP, ferry range and every other demand the officials could think of. Three of the partners' main aircraft companies did no more than study these requirements, and perhaps utter a low whistle;

Right: Three-view of Tornado IDS version, without FR probe fitted./*Panavia*

Below: The first model of MRCA to be exhibited in public, labelled Panavia 100, showed a single-seater without fixed wing gloves and with inlets omitted for security reasons. The date was September 1969./*Author*

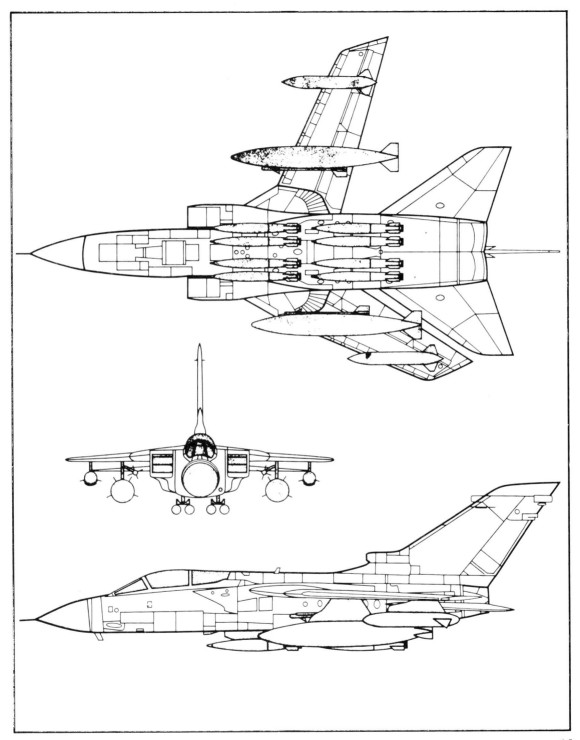

15

but BAC, MBB and Canadair submitted design proposals the following month. All had two engines, a VG wing and a conventional tail. It did not appear impossible to knock these submissions into one common type.

Had there been a United States of Europe in 1968 its government would undoubtedly have come to the conclusion that the aircraft that became Tornado was right for Europe. As it was, the separate national governments and air staffs never completely agreed on a single set of requirements, and three of the six starters dropped out entirely. First to leave was Belgium, never a strong participant nor apparently much concerned over bad weather and the blasting of its airfields, as witness its purchase of the F-104G, Mirage 5BA and F-16. Next to leave was Canada, not because it necessarily disagreed with the collaborative discussions but because in 1968 its whole armed forces were being ripped apart and melded into a sanitized peacekeeping force whose commitments were still being worked out; it simply did not wish to pay the bill for air fares to take part in the discussions until it could see what aircraft, if any, it might need.

Whilst the participants were dwindling, like the Ten Little Nigger Boys, B.O. 'Ollie' Heath of BAC – who, more than any other single engineer, could be called 'Mr Tornado' – examined the challenge of the OEO and came to the conclusion the various national officials were not being entirely reasonable. To take typical conflicting design cases, they expected the aircraft to carry everything and do everything in all conditions, so that the same armour was needed in sea reconnaissance at night as in battlefield close-support by day, while the landing requirement was based on an airstrip so slippery it was obviously covered in ice despite the fact that reverse-thrust effectiveness was reduced by an extreme hot day! Arguments of this kind are not uncommon, but in this case there were two important results. The first was that Heath's suggestion that different missions made different demands, and that it should prove possible to allow for this in trading, say, avionics for armour, or fuel for weapons, implanted the idea of different versions of the same basic design. Second, drawing the various requirements pictorially – at first as a plot of SEP against mission radius, but later embracing other parameters – threw into sharp focus the fact that all the central requirements were common to all customers. This made certain national demands stand out like sore thumbs. At all times the national officials had emphasised the overriding need for minimal aircraft size and cost, and by trimming off all the more extreme projecting national demands, just like Procrustes lopping off the parts of his guests who did not fit his bed, the aircraft size and cost were reduced dramatically.

This alteration in the basic size of the aircraft – the Americans call it the 'rubber airplane' stage – meant that it was still to be some months before the engine parameters could be fixed. This was unfortunate, because in general engines take longer to develop than aircraft, and designing an engine specifically to meet the exact needs of a particular aircraft is likely to result in a mismatch in timing. In this case, though the all-new engine and all-new aircraft matured with a remarkable absence of real bother, there is no doubt the engine should have been started as a programme a year and a half before the aircraft instead of six months after it.

In what was in most respects the first single collaborative document, the Joint Working Group of officials drafted a Statement of Work on 19 December 1968 which described a set of requirements that the JIC (Joint Industrial Company) replied could not only be met but met with a design not very far from the target weight and price. Afterwards the officials confided that the acclaim with which they greeted the news was doubly sincere, because none of them had even dared to believe such a jumping-off point possible. Having accomplished this miracle, it was then a disappointment when, at the end of December 1968, the JIC produced not one joint design but two (had Canadair still been in, it would have been three).

BAC's Feasibility Study report showed a thoroughbred whose ancestry could be traced back in nearly 50 stages through ACA, UKVG and AFVG to the P.45. It naturally had a broad fuselage, wing placed nearly in the high position and drop-out engines. In sharp contrast MBB's Feasibility Study showed an aircraft strongly reminiscent of the AVS and NKF, with a narrow but deep fuselage, mid-mounted wing and pull-out engines. It so happened that the JIC spokesman at the time was Heath (it was a three-month oscillating assignment with his MBB counterpart, Helmut Langfelder), and he personally analysed the differences between the submissions. He demonstrated that almost all the contrasting features sprang from the wing height and pivot position. But was a head-on confrontation inevitable?

It is worth a separate paragraph at this point to explain that some people imagine a collaborative programme means majority votes, and the imposition of one party's will on another. This has been true of at least one programme with which I am familiar, but it is unusual and a bad way to work. At the start of the serious engineering collaboration, before MRCA had even been completely defined, it was emphatically agreed that, on any matter of real importance, neither the top programme managers nor the technical staff would ever take a vote round the table. Instead, the problem and the various options would be talked through carefully until a decision had been reached that was unanimous. Someone once quipped that 'a camel is a horse designed by a committee', but in fact this is the only way to operate. It is the way decisions are taken in most programmes run by the giant US aerospace companies. A policy of decisions based on unanimous conviction is hard to beat.

January 1969 was the month in which not just the negotiating teams but the main design staffs really got down to detailed work. In February 1969 a large team of MBB, Fokker and Fiat engineers came to bleak Warton, and, because they were the men they were, the nitty-gritty discussions and arguments did not lead to cooled relations but to a mellowing of attitudes. By carefully avoiding rigid postures, or hard lines on the drawings, most of the problems were eased. It was the in-depth involvement that helped avoid the sharply focussed NIH (not invented here) outlook that often characterises small project teams. Instead each side was able to see the advantages underlying the other's solutions. In particular there were many MBB engineers with engine-installation responsibilities who actually preferred BAC's configuration, because their objective of drop-out engines was difficult to achieve with the fuselage frames needed with a mid-wing and low tailplane. Compatibility was also assisted by BAC's decision, stemming from the reduced aircraft size following the abandonment of east-of-Suez involvement, to move the wing pivots from inside the fuselage (where they had been on AFVG) to a location well outboard. The resulting fixed wing-root glove, or nib, helped meet the demand for ever-higher combat manoeuvrability. Gradually the central problem of wing location was resolved around the BAC configuration, and everything else pretty much fell into place. In March there was a big engineering meeting in Munich which concluded on the 14th with the submission of the second miracle: the Baseline Configuration brochure, showing a single aeroplane agreed by all partners.

This proposal was based on the RB.199 engine, because this was the only candidate engine for which figures were available. A few days later General Electric made available engine data which were at once used in a fresh submission called Annex A. Before the end of the month the RB.199 had been improved, and the new figures were submitted on 28 March as Annex B. Two days earlier, on 26 March 1969, the JIC had been formally constituted as a single multi-national company, Panavia GmbH, registered in Munich (actually in the offices of the defunct EWR) ready to receive the contract for the aircraft which had become known as the MRCA (Multi-Role Combat Aircraft).

It really was a double miracle that, in an environment of antipathetic politicians and strong nationalistic passions, such an emotive thing as a major new combat aircraft should have been agreed by three nations to meet their own requirements (indeed, at that time the Dutch were still in, so the number of partners was four). And it may be a third miracle that the aeroplane shown in the Baseline brochure in March 1969 is almost identical to the Tornado in service today. Apart from a minor change in wing-tip shape before the design was frozen, slight stiffening of the main landing-gear brackets, a couple of feet on the fuselage to get in a dual set of flight controls (again before freezing the design), extremely small modifications at the rear to obtain optimum flow, and a final small kink in the tailplane leading edge to accommodate the effect of particularly large underwing stores, the two designs look alike.

Right: Proof of the pudding: after all the years of toil GT.001 is inspected by the new Luftwaffe Chief of Staff, Gen Obleser, and Lt-Gen Tom Stafford, DCoS of the USAF, in July 1979./*MBB*

Basic Design

Most aircraft buffs have at least a general idea of why modern combat aircraft are not all the same shape. They know, for example, that an air-combat fighter must have the largest possible wing in order to achieve the minimum turn radius, while the ground-attack aeroplane must have the smallest possible wing in order that neither the aircraft nor crew shall be shaken to bits. Supersonic machines must obviously have minimum frontal area, a relatively thin wing and the smallest possible span. To make life harder, STOL performance naturally calls for the largest possible wing span, with slats and flaps which are impossible to fit on a traditional fixed-geometry supersonic wing. There are an almost infinite number of variables, most of which interact upon each other. The only variable upon which all partners agreed was to use two engines.

Another early agreement was to use tandem seating in any two-seat version, though despite strong pressure from the RAF and German Marineflieger this was at first regarded as a special variant for these users only. This meant that detailed planning of the cockpit could begin at the very start, in the spring of 1969, and this was important because everyone expected this to be a subject fraught with violent disagreement. In many – possibly the majority – of European military jets the cockpit was the subject of a last-minute panic. Uniquely, with this programme the four customer services thoroughly aired the problem right at the start, reached almost complete agreement on all major matters and by 1970 approved a detailed mock-up with the only arguments centering on the lettering of panels. Another area where work had to press ahead at full speed concerned systems and suppliers, because an exceptionally large and closely knit industrial structure had to be created involving not only the European partners but also the United States.

Right: This close-up of aircraft 03 (being studied by Canadian aircrew, assisted by David Eagles, right) shows the installed flight-refuelling probe./*BAe*

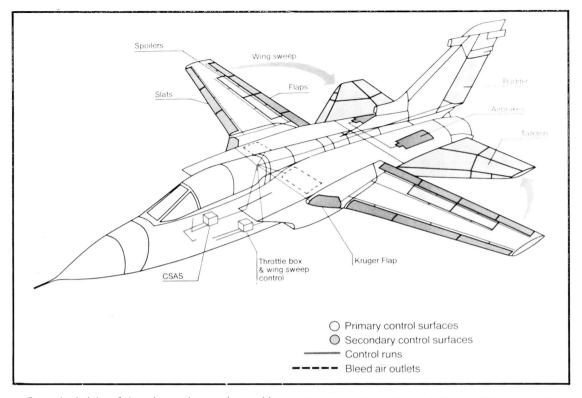

Spoilers

Wing sweep

Slats

Flaps

Rudder

Airbrakes

Taileron

Throttle box
& wing sweep
control

Kruger Flap

CSAS

○ Primary control surfaces
◑ Secondary control surfaces
── Control runs
▬ ▬ ▬ Bleed air outlets

Once the height of the wing and spanwise position of the pivot had been agreed, the basic shape of the aircraft caused little argument. MBB agreed with BAC that there had to be a large difference between the height of the wing and tailplane, to minimise interaction and the forcing of one surface by flow over the other (this was one of the features BAC could not understand on the original F-111). The wing box was placed above the unbroken fuselage centre-section, and a way was found to run strong longerons across above the longitudinal slits on each side at the rear for the wings in the fully swept position. The tailplane could then be located high enough, roughly mid-way up the fuselage, for the lower portions of the strong rear frames to be detachable for drop-out engine changing. There was no trouble in running the engine inlet ducts under the wing box, nor in finding room for the main landing gear further down, without cutting into the vital broad belly that (again unlike the F-111) was to be festooned with weapons.

I must emphasise that, right up to the late stage of collaborative analysis in the winter 1968-9, there were parallel studies into how the requirements might be met by a design having a fixed wing. All the basic design studies with a VG wing had shown that, in the standard plot of thrust/weight ratio against wing

Above: Simple diagram showing the Tornado flight-control surfaces with wings at 16°./*Panavia*

Above right: Secondary flight controls are operated chiefly by interlocked wing-sweep and high-lift levers./*Panavia*

Right: The primary flight-control system in diagrammatic form, emphasising the number of electronic boxes that process the pilot inputs./*Panavia*

loading, there was a rather small triangular area in which a successful design could be created. Its upper boundary was governed by radius of action, the lower boundary by the required SEP for the necessary flight performance, and the right-hand edge by the limiting wing loading for manoeuvre and extreme-g pull-out. (Any relaxation in any of the requirements would in most cases merely have brought in another line, due to a different cause, to limit the size of the triangle.) It was extremely significant that all the design teams found that the only possible triangle for a fixed-geometry aircraft occurred at a considerably greater weight. Of course, in some cases the refinement of a lighter VG aircraft means that it costs if anything more than the heavy one, but in general the heavier

20

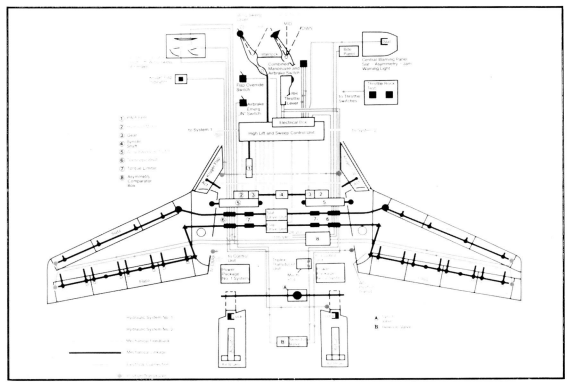

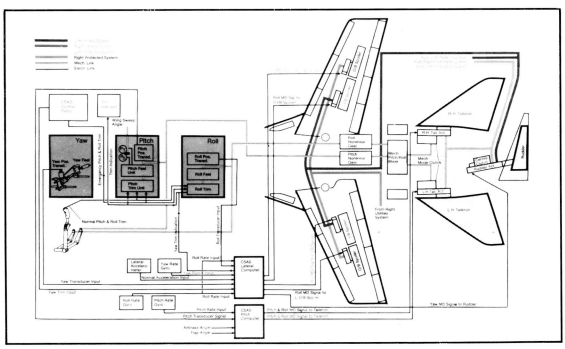

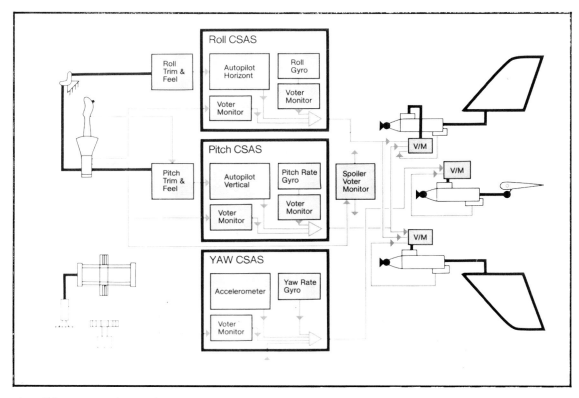

Roll CSAS

| Roll Trim & Feel | Autopilot Horizont | Roll Gyro |
| Voter Monitor | Voter Monitor |

Pitch CSAS

| Pitch Trim & Feel | Autopilot Vertical | Pitch Rate Gyro |
| Voter Monitor | Voter Monitor |

Spoiler Voter Monitor

V/M

V/M

V/M

YAW CSAS

| Accelerometer | Yaw Rate Gyro |
| Voter Monitor |

aircraft is more costly; and inevitably, for equal SEP, it must have bigger engines and burn more fuel. I emphasise this point because prolonged propaganda against Tornado by the media has left a vague impression that it ought not to have swing wings, and is thus foolishly complex. The answer is that it could be built with a fixed wing, if one accepted an aircraft that was larger, heavier, rougher to fly and used considerably more fuel.

Part of the emphasis on achieving absolute minimum dimensions was to make the fuselage short. The basic demand to carry a large multi-mode radar with a scanner of a certain large size naturally dictated the body cross-section, and this resulted in capacious cockpits with large side consoles and ample room for an exceptional array of systems, avionics and combat equipment, as well as (in the original design) all the fuel. This facilitated the attainment of minimum length, resulting in a large tail in order to retain the necessary control power. This was a deliberate objective, because, following experience with the much longer TSR.2, the British designers wished to use the tailplane not only for pitch, with left and right surfaces driven together, but also for roll. This means building what is popularly called a taileron, with left and right surfaces capable of being driven in opposite directions, and the

advantage of this is that it eliminates the need for ailerons and thus frees the entire trailing edge of the wing for high-lift flaps. This is especially important to a VG aircraft, which scores doubly over the fixed-sweep wing in being able to achieve an extremely high lift coefficient with the wings spread out at minimum sweep. Figures cannot be given, but the very small wing of Tornado can generate lift at low speeds (at take-off and landing) similar to that of supersonic fixed-geometry wings of twice the size. This is a factor sometimes not appreciated by people who compare one aircraft with another. Even the usually perceptive magazine *Flight International* completely overlooked this crucial fact in a major analysis that concluded the F-18 Hornet must be a better combat aircraft. In practical terms it enables Tornado to carry a bomb load considerably greater than a Lancaster, and from a shorter airfield.

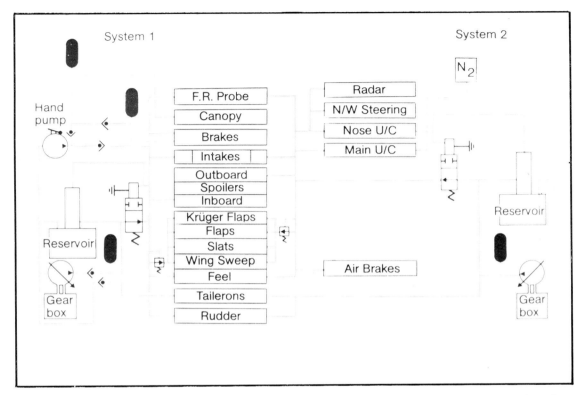

System 1

Hand
pump

F.R. Probe
Canopy
Brakes
Intakes
Outboard
Spoilers
Inboard
Krüger Flaps
Flaps
Slats
Wing Sweep
Feel
Tailerons
Rudder

Reservoir

Gear
box

System 2

N₂

Radar
N/W Steering
Nose U/C
Main U/C

Air Brakes

Reservoir

Gear
box

Structurally the Tornado is almost surprisingly conventional. In my view, it is mildly unfortunate that the structural design was settled just too early to make full use of the technology of fibre-reinforced composites which have been obvious ever since the Royal Aircraft Establishment at Farnborough started the story of modern carbon and graphite fibres in 1966. Despite intense and prolonged study, which fill the author's shelves with reports, the European R&D process persistently just misses taking advantage of the really significant advances, so that we find graphite composites throughout the structure of modern American fighters only — and with no evident increase in their technical risk. Tornado has CFRP (carbon-fibre reinforced plastics) in the tailerons; apart from this it is virtually all light alloy, and is almost indistinguishable from such machines as the early Century-series fighters of 1951-53 in having machined forgings, chemical- and machine-milled integrally stiffened skins and honeycomb-stabilized structure in the tailplanes and other movable surfaces. The central member of the wing, sometimes called the carry-through box or torque box, the structural heart of the aircraft, is electron-beam welded in titanium alloy. The advanced EBW joints introduce virtually no inbuilt stress and are ideal for long safe life, unlike the bolted joints of

some other VG aircraft. The quadruple Teflon pivot, which takes wing bending and twist, is backed up by sliding shear pads running on circular tracks, a solution proved in prolonged testing even before the start of the programme.

Standard range of sweep angles is 25° to 68°, controlled by an hydraulic motor driving a separate ballscrew on each side of the aircraft centreline. The F-14 Tomcat, an aircraft similar in many respects, has automatically controlled sweep, and it is rather surprising that this was not asked for by Tornado's customers. In some missions, especially those involving air combat, the need to keep inching the wings forward or back significantly adds to pilot workload, and I suspect auto-sweep will eventually be retrofitted, at least on the Tornado F2 (ADV).

One area where everyone can bask in their achievement is flight controls, where, either because of or in spite of the very latest technology, the result is truly marvellous. Prime contractor is Fairey, one of the few companies able to tackle such a task and turn in a superior performance. The system is triplexed — quad for the tailerons — with majority voting to cut out a failed channel. Signalling is by electrical fly-by-wire via a CSAS (command/stability augmentation system) which compares pilot demand voltages sensed by potentiometer pick-offs on the cockpit controls, feedback positions from the surface power units and pitch/roll/yaw rate signals sensed by gyros. The CSAS also ties in the autopilot and the artificial-feel system, to give a neat all-electric system governing the hydraulic surface units. Except for the rudder, two errors on any channel automatically cut out the fly-by-wire and clutch-in a mechanical drive direct from the cockpit to the surface power units.

Movable surfaces are primarily the tailerons and one-piece rudder. At low speeds at minimum sweep the wing movable surfaces can also be brought into play: Krüger flaps on the fixed inboard gloves, three-piece powered leading-edge slats, four-piece trailing-edge flaps (double-slotted, fixed-vane type) and two-section upper-surface spoilers. The spoilers can be used to augment the rate of roll at intermediate (combat) sweep angles, and also serve as lift dumpers after touchdown. A powerful door-type airbrake is recessed into the fuselage upper surface on each side of the fin.

All these items are naturally powered by the 4,000lb/sq in hydraulic system, energised by two pumps as described in the next chapter. This system also serves the wing-sweep actuators, landing gear, nose-leg extension and steering, canopy, FR probe, main radar scanner, laser retraction, brakes and inlet variable ramps. Fuel is housed in two main fuselage groups of self-sealing cells with provision for reticulated foam for explosion-suppression. Each cell-group has twin booster pumps able to feed both engines in full afterburner at sea level. The wings naturally need integral skins because of the full-span high-lift devices, but were originally to have been empty except in the case of RAF aircraft where wet wings were essential. In 1970 the decision was taken to use wet wings throughout, each wing (and a very substantial volume of optional external fuel) feeding by electric transfer pumps into the fuselage.

Tornado's internal fuel capacity is exceptionally large for an aircraft of such modest dimensions, and three 1,500-litre (330 Imp gal, 396 US gal) drop tanks can be carried. But a flight-refuelling probe was a requirement for the RAF, and so the IDS aircraft was designed to accept a neatly packaged probe which can be attached in a fairing on the outside of the right side just below the canopy. The probe itself lies alongside the windscreen, and on pilot command can be extended hydraulically from a hinge just ahead of the canopy/screen joint. The fairing behind this point covers the fuel supply pipe. IDS Tornados for other customers have provision for probe units but these are not supplied. (The ADV fighter Tornado has a probe fitted internally because it was designed for RAF requirements.)

As noted later, the British-led pressure for more and more fuel even led to a wet fin, but the low consumption of the amazingly small engines made it unnecessary to separate them by the width of the forward fuselage and fill the intervening space with integral tanks, as is necessary in the F-14 Tomcat. Such a layout was assessed in 1968-9, but it gave no benefits. Thus the forward fuselage tapers away as the inlet ducts sweep inwards to meet the tightly packed engines. This puts the two nozzles close together and facilitates linking the engines to a cross-shaft driving the SPS (secondary power system). But seen from underneath, the disappearance of the fuselage is masked by the outward sweep of the undersurface to provide adequate track for the main landing gear and accommodation for its retraction. The inlets sweeping in and the undersurface sweeping out is unique, though it is seen in a mild form on Jaguar.

The resulting broad flat belly unencumbered by main landing gears did not happen by chance; it was from the start one of the Tornado's central assets, achieved by designers who even had the temerity to point out the lack of it in the TFX (F-111) long before that aircraft had flown. It was a basic objective of the design engineers to try to hang all the external loads on the fuselage, leaving the wings clean as long as possible. At first the datum weapon carriage specified by the customers was modest, but the more experienced engineers predicted that this happy situation would not last. They were right; by 1974 the pattern had emerged, with the Tornado eventually being required to carry a greater weight and variety of external stores than any other known type of tactical aircraft. The list includes virtually every recent-past, present and future type of external weapon, tank, reconnaissance pod, ECM payload, flare and other load of all four customers. At first these filled the wide belly; then they encroached on the wings as an overload, and ultimately they filled the wings as a permanent fit. Taken in conjunction with the very considerable increase in internal fuel capacity, the result was a major rise in take-off weight which greatly enhances mission capability without increasing the size of the aircraft. Refinement in lift and propulsion to meet the increasing weight remains available to boost flight performance in the clean configuration.

From the start all customers were agreed on the need for an internal gun (which they probably would not have been ten years earlier). There were some obvious possible choices, but the decision was taken in 1971 to develop a new gun in Germany under direct contract. The IKWA Mauser-Werke at Oberndorf, which in World War II had pioneered the revolver cannon, undertook to meet the demand for a gun offering high muzzle velocity, high rate of fire from the first round, identical ballistics for all of several types of ammunition, fuses that unfailingly worked at very acute grazing angles, and minimum recoil on the air-

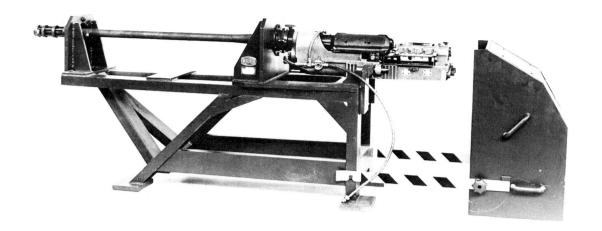

frame, as well as such obvious demands as high reliability. The resulting gun has a calibre of 27mm and weighs 100kg (220lb), and is self-powered to either a high rate of fire (air-to-air) or an optimised lower rate (air-to-ground). Diehl and Dynamit-Nobel produce the five types of electrically ignited ammunition. The standard aircraft has two of these guns, designated MK27 (Maschinen Kanone), in the lower front fuselage.

These guns are outstanding in both the 'fighter' and 'attack' roles, and it is possible today to make good radars and even some weapons that can serve in either role. But there is inevitably a conflict between the single-seat air-superiority fighter, with a large fixed-geometry wing and large engine(s), and the two-seat attack aircraft filled with all-weather sensors and characterised by a small VG wing and small engines. Tornado is the best compromise for both missions that has ever been created, but at all times there have been strong forces pulling the design either one way or the other.

In the early days MRCA was regarded by the Luftwaffe and Italians as strictly a single-seater. It had relatively limited radius and endurance, and though it was intended to be a night and all-weather aircraft there were many experts, among both the customers and the contractors, who argued for a simpler and cheaper aircraft. During the definition phase in 1968 the British, reflecting the invariant requirement of the RAF, always fully respected the weight and volume for the most complete kit of avionics, whereas MBB, reflecting the slightly different philosophy of the Luftwaffe, were prepared to cut back on avionics in order to keep the aircraft weight and price within fixed limits. Again, the RAF were at first out on a limb in calling for two seats and wet wings, and it was at quite a late stage in 1970 that a two-seat version was formally admitted into the programme to meet the needs

of the RAF and Marineflieger. This naturally increased the overall bill for R&D, and it could have led to newspaper headlines of soaring costs and to cancellation of the whole project. Instead the national officials took a positive line and all concerned worked hard to save costs elsewhere by rationalising the radar fit (which had begun with four different customer variations) and reducing the number of jointly-specified weapon permutations.

Unlike Jaguar, where the two-seater has simpler avionics and equipment, the two-seat MRCA was associated with both a higher avionic weight and a greater radius. The latter was met by the wet wings, but the weight of the additional equipment and the second cockpit caused a balance problem which was neatly met by slightly altering the wing sweep angles, those for the two-seater being a few degrees less than for the light-nose single-seat version. This continued until 1974, the two versions by this time being distinguished by the numbers of 100 and 200 (thus, they were popularly called Panavia 100 and Panavia 200, the industrial consortium having been named Panavia as explained in a another chapter). But then a curious thing happened. The ease with which variable sweep accommodated a two-seater led to an agreement among all customers for a dual-control trainer version. To make room for the second set of flight controls about 20 inches were added to the fuselage, giving a new length for all versions. Acceptance of the trainer made the Germans look again at the pros and cons of a two-seater operational version, because it had always been the intention that the two-pilot variation should have almost complete operational capability.

At the same time there was a growing feeling in Germany that it was a mistake to accept a reduced avionic fit, one protagonist exclaiming 'Who can believe that in the 1980s Germany can manage with a daylight fighter?' After a prolonged and detailed study of likely European scenarios in the 1980s, it emerged clearly from the German study that the two-seater not only offered a more realistic cockpit workload but was actually the more cost/effective solution.

Accordingly, despite its slightly higher cost, the "British" forward fuselage with its tandem cockpits and top-grade avionics, was adopted by the Luftwaffe in preference to the lighter single-seat version. This gave almost total commonality with the variant for the Marineflieger; but the Italian Air Force, the third continental customer, and shown only secondary interest in the CAS or IDS roles. Yet, after studying the German report, the Italians also accepted the two-seat version as standard. Once the unwelcome outsider, the two-seater became the universal choice of all participants. The single-seater, like the parallel non-VG studies, was dropped from the programme, along with the redundant designations Panavia 100 and 200. An extremely high degree of commonality thus ensued between all versions, and it remains in the aircraft now in production. (Later a prominent German general gained world-wide publicity in a violent attack on Tornado in a TV programme, claiming – among other things – that the two-seater had been foisted on their partners by the British!)

The only major area remaining to be discussed in this chapter is avionics. I have to do more than just outline today's fit, because it did not arise without prolonged argument. Indeed, in the early days of the programme the designers and officials had to work hard preventing open confrontation between a Royal Air Force which had great experience with all-weather attack avionics and was determined with MRCA to create the greatest integrated system known to man, and a Luftwaffe which had grown up with the relatively simple Massive Retaliation F-104G and whose

thoughts revolved around the purchase and upkeep of 700 new aircraft whose price had to be kept to a minimum. Essentially, there was one school of thought primarily concerned with simplicity, low cost and reducing risk, and another almost diametrically opposed that wanted advanced technological skills for its people and an aircraft that would still be modern in 1990.

Of course, there was little dispute about navigation and cockpit displays: the main nav/attack computer and the autopilot/flight-director are both fed by an inertial system, and the main computer is also served by a doppler radar. The pilot has an HSI (horizontal situation indicator), HUD (head-up display, which presents data and other guiding symbols on the windscreen, focussed at infinity so that the pilot can read them while he studies the ground ahead) and a moving-map display. The navigator has a combined radar and moving-map display, and two TV tabs, which were announced to the world by a British Minister as tabulators but are actually tabular displays on which the back-seater can call up any information he needs. There are also such things as an air-data computer, UHF/ADF and an SAHR system – which in this case means secondary attitude and heading reference but in the missile field stands for semi-active homing radar, which could be confusing.

All these things are to be expected, but the subject today called 'offensive avionics' was bound to produce differences of opinion. Well used to the need for what the jargon calls 'blind first-pass attack', in other words for flying straight to a point target and hitting it even in thick fog at night, the RAF decided they wanted to have three sets of sensors, each with successively shorter EM (electromagnetic) wavelength, used consecutively. The outward flight was to be made using an I-band (called X-band in the old scheme) radar in the ground-mapping or terrain-following modes, terrain-following causing the aircraft automatically to hug the ground at the lowest safe height to try to escape detection by radar or being shot down by guns or mis-

Left: P.01 lined up ready to go, with wings in high-lift configuration and nose leg compressed as thrust builds./*Panavia*

Right: The first take-off, from Manching, on 14 August 1974. /*Panavia*

Below: The first air-to-air photograph, among low cloud on the first flight./*Panavia*

Bottom: After the 'official' first flight at Manching on 21 September 1974: from the left, 'Fred' Rammensee, German Defence Minister Georg Leber, Paul Millett, UK Defence Under-Secretary Brynmor John and Italian CAS Gen Dino Ciarlo./*MBB*

siles. Near the target a second radar was to take over, operating in J-band. When in line-of-sight range, a laser would be switched on for final precise ranging. For several years this three-tier system, to be produced mainly by Ferranti and Elliott in Britain, was expected to be fitted, but for cost reasons — as noted earlier in this chapter — was replaced by a simpler two-tier package which happened to give the United States a piece of the action which in time could prove politically helpful.

There were actually two American radars on offer. The one that appealed most strongly to the Germans, because of its futurisitc technology, was an electronically scanned set by Autonetics. But sheer price won the day for TI (Texas Instruments), which had previously produced the TFR (terrain-following radar) for the F-111. The TI radar may not be 1980s technology but it is a fair compromise and far better than anything previously used by Western European air forces. The big main scanner, which gives the aircraft its broad nose like its counterparts the F-111 and Su-19, has relatively low PRF (pulse-repetition frequency) and scans side-to-side in the ground mapping mode. Under it is the smaller aerial for the TFR, with high PRF, which as described later scans differently to guide the aircraft across the terrain with an invisible 'ski-toe' profile constantly nosing out hills or obstructions. A laser ranger/marked-target receiver is fitted in a retractable box under the nose. Today's Tornado has a less-advanced system than the RAF would have liked, and one about twice as advanced as the Luftwaffe thought it could accept. The result is thus about right.

Recently General Obleser, Chief of Staff of the Luftwaffe, listed the uniquely long list of requirements Tornado was designed to meet. He went on: 'Today, ten years after having drafted these requirements, we would hardly wish to alter them. I know of no other weapons system where the objectives and the manner in which they are met have remained so constant as in the case of the Tornado.'

27

Propulsion

Though some aircraft enthusiasts hardly give them a thought, engines are if anything even more important that the airframe. They take longer to develop, and in the case of Tornado were the central key to the amazingly small size of the eventual aircraft. Beyond doubt, the engines of Tornado are the most advanced in use anywhere in the world. With other engines the aircraft would be larger, slower, clumsier and shorter-ranged, the difference being multiplied by the fact that longer and less-efficient engines result in a much bigger and heavier aircraft.

During the 1967 study phase the former Bristol Siddeley (now Rolls-Royce) team at Patchway (Bristol) extrapolated beyond the M45G afterburning turbofan that had been intended to power AFVG, and also studied the Derby-developed technology of using three separate rotating spools, an LP (low-pressure), IP (intermediate) and HP (high). Pioneered in the RB.211 civil engine, this appears to make the engine complex but in fact makes it smaller – especially shorter – and, according to Rolls-Royce, actually reduces the number of parts. Each of the three spools can run at its own best speed without the need for extensive variable blading, and fewer stages are needed to achieve the desired pressure ratio. By 1968 there was no shadow of doubt that the three-shaft engine could beat any two-shaft design such as the M45G or the various American proposals.

At that time it was by no means certain that a new engine could happen. In my view some of the benefits of international collaboration – to a programme, as distinct from the obviously desirable erosion of purely national outlook – are overrated; a hard-driving one-nation programme, such as the Hawk, can move much faster than a multinational one. But in the case of Tornado the larger number of MRCAs spoken for by the partner nations provided a firm basis of planning with shared R&D costs and reduced unit prices, and the release of funds was calculated to be sufficient to support a completely new engine. This in turn was vital to the degree of success attained by the aircraft

designers. The existence of the outstandingly advanced and challenging new engine proposal at Bristol had two major results. It kept out any older-technology derivative engine proposed at lower price by anyone else; and it enabled the aircraft teams to crank in totally different figures to their calculations resulting in a much smaller and better aircraft. The difference was truly dramatic, and predictably most of it was used not so much in making the aircraft literally smaller externally as in making it bigger internally, in such matters as fuel capacity and weapon load. Today's Tornado is actually smaller than the AFVG would have been, but it does at least twice the job.

Incidentally, though twin engines were preferred for many well-rehearsed reasons, the customers would probably have been persuaded to accept a single engine had there been no evident alternative. The point is worth making because, like variable-sweep wings, no decision was taken blindly or without carefully studying the alternatives. If acceptance of an existing engine had been unavoidable the chance of a single-engine configuration would have been greater, with a further penalty in aircraft size and effectiveness, quite apart from the combat advantages of a twin.

In March 1969 the datum MRCA was defined, Panavia was formed, and an engine competition was held. This was not one of those competitions where the decision is taken in advance. The customers wanted the best aeroplane, and the submissions by the engine companies had to be worked into the datum aircraft with impartial accuracy because Panavia also wanted the best aircraft. It is fortunate that all three engine giants were involved. Pratt & Whitney did their utmost to promote the various advanced developments of the TF30, including the new JTF22 (later styled F100), and the paper JTF16, but none was quite matched to the requirement and the company was handicapped by US security and withdrew. General Electric perhaps tried harder, with the GE1/10; as noted earlier it made a formal submission, which was incorporated as Annex A to the Datum Proposal by Panavia. But the improved RB.199 was so demonstrably superior that the only thing I question is the failure to take a decision until 5 September 1969. On that date the RB.199-34R was formally selected, and on 30 September 1969 an international consortium was formed to produce it.

Though the basic design was done entirely at Patchway the partners in the engine programme were wholly responsible for detailed design, production and

Right: Preparing an -03 engine for installation in aircraft No 12, at Warton. There are substantial differences both internally and externally between different engine models./*Rolls-Royce*

Above: Painted royal blue, the simulated half-fuselage complete with engine and gun fitted neatly under the last Mk 1 Vulcan to remain in active status./*Rolls-Royce*

support of their own assigned parts. The consortium is called Turbo-Union Ltd, and its shareholding is Rolls-Royce and MTU 40% each and Fiat 20%. Its head office is at Bristol, but another office is at Munich next to Panavia. The precise division of work has varied slightly to maintain these percentages, and in any case has also been changed between design and produciton, but the production allocation is: Rolls-Royce, inlet and LP case, fan, combustion system, HP turbine complete, turbine casings, afterburner and fuel control system; MTU, IP and HP compressors, intermediate casing, accessory drive and gearbox, by-pass duct (outer engine casing), IP turbine and drive-shaft, and reverser; Fiat, LP turbine complete, LP drive-shaft, exhaust diffuser, rear jetpipe and variable nozzle.

Unlike the Tornado airframe the RB.199 was designed to use all the latest constructional technology. The three-stage fan, which was aerodynamically derived from the much larger fan of the Pegasus, is assembled by precision electron-beam welding (EBW), and the fan stators are also all-welded. The EBW construction saves weight compared with traditional insertion of separate blades, and also reduces vibration. Replacement of damaged blades by cutting and welding has been demonstrated. The IP compressor rotor, with three stages, is also an EBW structure, and it is driven by a single-stage aircooled turbine. There are no variable stators, the only airflow trimming control being an IP blow-off. The six-stage HP compressor is driven by a single-stage aircooled turbine as advanced as any in the world, with entry gas temperature of over 1,327°C at full power. This shaft also drives the accessories, which are on the underside for easy accessibility with the engine installed.

The combustion chamber is of the annular type, with vaporising burners. As noted later, this has been refined to give near-perfect combustion, and obviously the objective is to eliminate visible smoke. Downstream of the exhaust diffuser is what is in my view the best afterburner ever built. It was a basic requirement that the Tornado engine should have two distinct regimes of operation: maximum dry (non-afterburning) thrust with outstanding fuel economy for long-range interdiction, and very high augmented (afterburning) thrust for short take-off, Mach 2 speed and combat manoeuvre. The RB.199 afterburner gives record augmentation of approximately 100%, with fully modulated response to pilot demand, in an exceptionally small volume. The afterburner is a dual type, with an inner turbojet-style manifold and gutter flameholder, and an outer burner in the fan airflow, separately fuelled, with a colander-type flameholder based on experience with Bristol's ramjets and PCB (plenum-chamber burning) systems.

The nozzle is also outstanding. People knowing little about engines have commented how beautifully it seems to fit the back-end of the aircraft, with minimal base area in the dry regime. Its perfectly profiled overlapping petals are driven by a translating (fore/aft sliding) outer shroud positioned by four screwjacks. Integral with it is the reverser, whose upper and lower target clamshells fit flush when housed, but quickly swing out and back to deflect the jets diagonally forward above and below the fuselage. Both the nozzle and reverser are driven by fireproof pneumatic motors running on HP bleed air.

Turbo-Union met severe demands with the SPS (secondary power system). Most unusually, the two engines are linked via their gearboxes to a cross-shaft which is automatically engaged should the engine speeds differ by more than a specified limit; thus, either engine can drive all secondary-power supplies. Each gearbox carries a hydraulic pump, IDG

Above: Official handover of the engines for the first production aircraft, BT.001, at Warton in early May 1979. From left: B. O. Heath, Panavia director of systems engineering (and a mainspring behind the whole programme from its inception); F. G. Willox, BAe Tornado executive director; H. Francis, Turbo-Union manager at Warton; J. T. Froud, BAe chief project engineer (propulsion); and J. Sweet, assistant Turbo-Union manager. Note close view of final nib fairing under rudder./*BAe*

Left: Once the accessory module is in place the rest of the engine is assembled vertically. Here two fitters at MTU Munich-Allach put finishing touches to one of the engines for GT.001. Note the almost fully opened reverser buckets at the top./*MTU*

(integrated constant-speed drive generator) for electric power, oil pump and HP fuel pump. Engine and gearbox oil is cooled by an oil/fuel heat exchanger, the hot fuel then either going to the engine or, if the fuel demand is small (as it always is with an RB.199 in dry power), back to the tanks via an air-cooling radiator. The right gearbox also carries a KHD APU (auxiliary power unit), a small gas turbine rated at 114kW (153hp) which starts the main engines by air bleed and can provide full system power throughout the airframe – on the ground or in the air – without having to run either main engine. Tornados engaged in certain trials which could risk flameout of both engines (such as spinning) have also been fitted with a hydrazine EPU (emergency power unit).

Turbo-Union were keenly aware of the fact that full go-ahead on the engine came six months after the aircraft, instead of the ideal 18 or more months ahead of it. This, and the sheer importance of the programme, prompted the use of a flying test-bed (FTB). The chosen aircraft was the Vulcan previously used as the FTB for the Concorde engine and thus already suitable with stressing and instrumentation for a large belly pod. Aeritalia and Marshalls jointly made a near-representation of the left half of an MRCA body with a functioning variable inlet and dummy reverser, and eventually preceded by an MK27 cannon in the correct relative position. While this major installation was being built, prototype engines began to appear to RB.199-01 standard and the first made a successful run on the bench at Patchway on 27 September 1971. Further prototypes ran at Bristol, Munich and Turin during the following year, and on 19 April 1973 the chief test pilot of Rolls-Royce, John Pollitt, under contract to Turbo-Union, began flight development in the Vulcan. This aircraft gradually explored behaviour up to 50,000ft/Mach 0.92, while simulated Mach 2 flight was investigated in a supersonic test cell at the National Gas Turbine Establishment at Pyestock.

Performance targets agreed for the -01 engine were well short of the production figures. In the period 1971-6 Turbo-Union transformed engine performance through four series of development engines, culminating in the -04 which is virtually the same as the production powerplant. The first major improvement, the -02, achieved increased thrusts at all regimes with no increase in gas temperature, chiefly by opening out the annulus area between the IP and LP turbine stator blades to give a greater core airflow. This was an important engine and a few were still flying in 1979. The -03 introduced broader fan blades to cure a flutter problem at high rpm in one part of the flight envelope, and other changes to give higher thrust; these engines entered the flight programme in March 1977. In 1978 the -03 powered most Tornado flying, but the main engine on the test-bed was the -04, with further refinements, which entered the Tornado flight programme in March 1978 and led direct to the Mk 101 production engine.

This development programme has in the main been highly successful, and has resulted in an engine significantly more powerful – and superior in other ways – to that offered in the brochure of March 1969. But there have also been problems, and though these have been trivial compared with those of the engines of the American F-111, F-14 and F-15, which have caused great concern for more than a decade, they have gained such publicity that they must be outlined here. By far the most serious difficulty was the shedding of HP turbine blades. Even with blades missing, but contained, the RB.199 is such a smooth engine that this has never been noticed until revealed by post-flight inspection, and on one occasion an engine was cycled through 20 hours of simulated

combat flying with missing blades to see what happened (answer: nothing). Unfortunately, what did impact on the Tornado programme was the elusive nature of the cure, which was eventually traced to causes involving the internal air cooling and resonance which resulted in interference between the tip shrouds.

Another prolonged but much less serious problem was surging, or violently unstable breakdown of air and gas flow within the engine. This leads to sharply varying engine behaviour, and in older engines often resulted in catastrophic breakup of the engine (but never in an RB.199). Surging is obvious from the explosive sounds emitted from an affected engine, and the problem eased somewhat with the introduction of the -03 series; in late 1977 R. P. Beamont, the famous test pilot who then was director of Panavia flight-test, summed it up by saying 'We don't hear so many morning duck-shoots as we used to'. The only other snags worth mentioning were poor oil supply to the gearbox (soon cured), the failure of the original electronic MECU (main-engine control unit) to meet the specification (it was replaced by a new MECU family by Rolls-Royce which subsequently were assigned to an outside supplier to produce) and the very obvious generation of smoke. Surprisingly, smoke was not mentioned in the original engine specification, but after the Yom Kippur war in 1973 everyone woke up to what tactical pilots had known for years and eventually the Tornado was made absolutely smokeless.

This wholly exceptional piece of miniaturized turbomachinery provides an outstanding foundation for the Tornado programme. While on one hand Turbo-Union has discussed other applications with both Panavia and several other aircraft companies, the Tornado itself could well use later versions of this engine. As described later, the RAF wishes to stick with the Mk 101 in its Tornado F2 air-defence version, but the Germans and Italians are interested in engines of thrust even greater than the enhanced levels offered by the Mk 101. As this book went to press no decision had been taken on increased-thrust versions, though these are clearly defined and could be not only introduced to production rather painlessly but also produced by field kits for modifying engine modules with the squadrons.

Right: January 1978 line-up at Manching showing the first five German prototypes, including much-modified 01 with its new number 98/04 (note its sooty fin from reverser trials)./*MBB*

The Programme

By the start of 1969 the general form of MRCA had been finalised, though still with single-engined and fixed-wing studies as comparative yardsticks; and it had been agreed that the design, development and manufacture would be shared by all participating nations. There was to be no 'design leader' – that emotive factor so unimportant to the actual work of the engineers yet such a stumbling-block in programmes between Britain and France – but it was agreed that BAC Warton would be responsible for the two-seat variant, then planned only for the RAF and Marineflieger, while single-seaters were to be managed from Munich. Each partner in the airframe programme was to assemble the aircraft for his own country, and accept particular responsibilities in the flight-test programme.

When Panavia was formed on 26 March 1969 it was a four-nation company. BAC and MBB each held one-third of the shares, and Fiat and Fokker-VFW one-sixth. The Definition Phase started on 1 May 1969, and 14 days later the governments of Germany, Italy and the UK signed a Memorandum of Understanding pledging to co-operate in the definition, with the expectation it would be followed by design, development and production. (It is worth noting that the entire programme was, probably wisely, agreed by the participating governments stage-by-stage. At the end of each phase any country could have withdrawn.) The Netherlands did not sign, and on 28 July 1969 Lt-Gen Willem den Toom, Dutch Defence Minister, announced his country's withdrawal. He said MRCA was too complex and expensive (in effect he was saying Holland had no need for aircraft able to make a pinpoint attack in bad weather) and that, as it could not be ready until 'well after 1975' it was too late for the RNethAF. (In fact the eventual choice, the F-16, was not even selected until 1975, for service later than Tornado.) This knocked 100 aircraft out of the programme, and the tail unit went to BAC instead of the Fokker works at Amsterdam.

Panavia redistributed its national shares so that BAC and MBB each hold 42.5% and Aeritalia (as Fiat airframe division had become) 15%. The full name of the company is Panavia Aircraft GmbH, a typical bilingual construction, and its office is in the former EWR building in fashionable Bogenhausen, on the outskirts of Munich. Panavia acts as the single trinational supplier of Tornado, and of course hopes to create other aircraft in the fulness of time. It does not actually do the work itself, but has a staff that began at 90 and grew to nearly 300 technically qualified managers, mathematicians and accountants. One of their tasks is to run the programme so that flow of money across partner frontiers is minimised, and if possible eliminated.

For their part, the three governments set up a similar single customer, called NAMMO (NATO MRCA Management Organisation) made up of the senior executives – uniformed and civilian – controlling the programme for each government. NAMMO's policy decisions have been carried out by the organisation's executive branch, NAMMA (A for agency), with a large staff of specialists skilled in such matters as advanced aircraft technology, military operations, international contract law and various political considerations. NAMMA was accommodated in the same building as Panavia. One could argue interminably about the housing of officials and company staff under one roof, but in this programme it has probably saved months of time and millions of pounds. This centralised control on both the customer and supplier sides has worked outstandingly well, and has demonstrated its superiority over the arrangements in past collaborative programmes.

Left: Shrouded in secrecy, aircraft 01 is about to make its first journey, at midnight, from the Ottobrunn assembly hangar to the test airfield at Manching on 12 November 1973./*MBB*

Overleaf
Top left: Tornado P-06, carrying finned ECM pods on swivelling pylons under the outer wing panels, flying over Wales./*Richard Wilson*

Bottom left: Last pre-production aircraft, No 16, at intermediate sweep with Kormorans./*MBB*

Top right: Pre-production aircraft 13 with MW-1 dispenser, four-waveband ECM pod and, on the near wing, an unexplained store with small horizontal wings, four diagonal vortex generators and flat boat-tail./*MBB*

Bottom right: Italian prototype 09 flying over the Mediterranean with five bombs and two ECM pods, the latter being of an unidentified type with no ventral inlet but with four lateral aerials presumably for different frequency bands; note also small bulge under right side of nose./*Aeritalia*

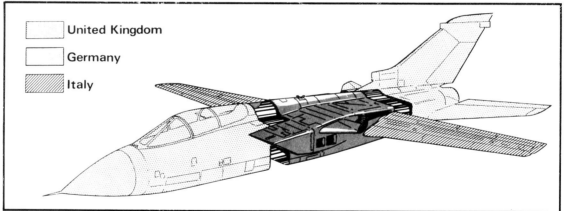

United Kingdom

Germany

Italy

Panavia is prime contractor for the entire Tornado weapon system, including all its parts. To manage the obviously extensive avionics a tri-national company was formed on 26 September 1969 called Avionics System Engineering GmbH, with one-third of the shares each assigned to Easams (UK), ESG (Germany) and SIA (Italy). In 1971 this arrangement was replaced by a straightforward prime subcontract to Easams at Camberley, which in turn placed work-sharing subcontracts with ESG and SIA, as well as to itself. The three partners formed two tri-national engineering groups, CDMT (Central Design and Management Team) based at Easams and IST (International Software Team) at Munich. IST had a big enough job writing the computer programmes, but

CDMT had the monumental task of writing and sending out to possible suppliers the detailed specifications for the 50-odd major avionic equipment items. For its part, NAMMA had the job of choosing the various suppliers, and this was a giant task.

Some of the countless difficulties can be explained. The first essential was to decide what the aircraft had to carry in the way of avionics in order to fly its missions, and each customer had his own ideas; in fact, often there simply had to be national fits, so that, for example, Italy could fire Aspide missiles, the RAF its Martels, the Luftwaffe streuwaffen or MW-1 cluster-bombs and the Marineflieger Kormoran missiles. Then a delicate balance had to be struck between the newest advanced-technology ideas and the older, but proven

Far left, top: Warton, 30 October 1974, and aircraft 02 gets airborne for the first time. Main gears have single wheels of modest size, but footprint pressure is low (CBR figure is 10) enabling Tornado to use unpaved strips./*BAe*

Far left, bottom: Simple diagram showing who builds what./*Panavia*

Left: White vortices stream from the tips of 01 in the high-lift configuration./*Image in Industry*

Below: Another view of 01; in the thousands of parts of this first three-nation aircraft there was only one error, soon rectified: six rivets were domed instead of being countersunk./*Image in Industry*

Overleaf
Left: Near-stern view of 03 with Kormorans and Ajax pods, with original non-standard fin camera replaced by passive aerial but with nine fin vortex-generators. Note outward sweep of inlet duct./*BAe*

Right: First prototype of the Tornado ADV, the F2, which was ceremoniously rolled out at BAe Warton on 9 August 1979 and made its first flight on 27 October./*BAe*

Above: Hanover show 1978, with 04 on display with weapons; in the foreground Panavia managing director Dr Peter Fichtmüller and flight-test crews hand out autographed photos./*MBB*

Left: Another weapon display, this time around 08 at Farnborough, 1978, with double crowd barrier (really needed on the public days!). /*BAe*

and available, 'black boxes' which would reduce the technical risk. Then Panavia and NAMMA had to study carefully all the hundreds of possible suppliers, not leaving out the United States, taking note of their past track-record, technical expertise and available products. Some had fine products, but which were likely to pose compatibility problems when integrated with dozens of others in the close-knit Tornado system. Then a careful check had to be made on the proposed groupings, each main avionics supplier – like the companies selected to build the landing gear, variable inlets, cockpit canopy and everything else – having to team up with partners in the three participating countries in order to achieve the correct work-split.

But even this only scratches the surface of the problem. There is such a thing as commercial security; people have gone to prison for unlawfully disclosing a company's jealously guarded advanced-technology

secrets to a commercial rival. How could a company bid for a piece of the Tornado action without disclosing its latest secrets? If it lost, it had done so to no purpose. If it won the position might be even worse, because it would have to tell the secrets to foreign rivals in such detail that they could take a full part in the manufacturing programme. And how could Panavia and NAMMA be sure that a large and old company might turn in a better performance than a bright young team with no track-record but strong motivation and a lot of up-to-date talent? Time after time the officials and managers worked right round the clock trying to take what seemed to be the best decisions. It was not just the work-sharing but the

Overleaf

Top left: Prototype 06 was the first to fire its MK 27mm guns, at both the selectable rates of fire./*BAe*

Bottom left: Colourful 05 was flown solo by Pietro Paolo Trevisan from Turin Caselle on 5 December 1978, the rear cockpit being filled with instrumentation./*Aeritalia*

Top right: First take-off of aircraft 14, still in epoxy primer paint, flown by Quarantelli and Nappi; note forward-facing oblique camera instead of EW passive receiver aerial near top of fin, also fitted to 03 during first few flights./*Aeritalia*

Bottom right: Prototype 04 on display at Hanover in 1978 in MFG colours, with cockpit interior shrouded for security./*MBB*

expertise-sharing that caused the heated arguments, yet in literally scores of cases ways were found to get companies that had been bitter rivals, and which had never before collaborated with anyone, to pool their ideas, their design talent and their total resources to make the Tornado programme work the way it was intended on a tri-national basis. And I cannot think of a single one of these partnerships – even the ones created under duress – that has not worked well, delivered the goods, and will endure even into quite different programmes, to the lasting benefit of Europe and probably the world.

But back in 1969-71 it was a real slog, and often nobody could be sure that a viable network of suppliers could ever be created. Some observers got quite agitated about it. On 29 September 1971 a British MP wrote to *The Times:* 'The Germans and Italians are committed to supplying $57\frac{1}{2}\%$ of the capacity required. In the equipment area they cannot produce even half of this from their existing resources. So, mostly after buying expensive licences from the United States, they are going to build new factories, recruit new workers and train them, while here in Britain our skilled, unemployed men and machines are

Above left: Celebrating the 1,000th test flight; Fichtmüller has the bottle and the ciné camera is held by the general manager of NAMMA, General H. Birkenbeil, former head of Luftwaffe procurement and noted test pilot; flanking him are Fritz Soos and Kurt Schreiber./*MBB*

Left: E. Hils, quality-control officer for the German Defence Ministry at MBB Augsburg, signs the release documents for the first production centre fuselage now flying in BT.001/*MBB*

Above: Structural heart of the Tornado, the centre fuselage is produced at MBB's Augsburg factory, site of the original BFW and Messerschmitt company headquarters. The fuselage nearest the camera has yet to receive the welded-titanium wing centre box. /*MBB*

Right: Construction of new floor space is a rare thing in British Aerospace, but this new assembly hall was completed at Warton in 1979 for the Tornado programme/*BAe*

forced to stand idle and watch . . .' He went on to cast the United States in the role of a villainous commercial rival who, via the inexperienced Germans and Italians, was poised to get in as lowest bidder on all the MRCA avionics and then escalate the price. In truth, it was not quite like this, and the powerful industrial team that resulted was just about the best that could be devised. The only adverse factor was that the sheer size of the task of sorting out the avionics and other equipment items set the timing back by about six months. (With a bit of long-range vision, this industrial network can serve as the foundation for future European programmes, so we need not go through it all again.)

Compared with this, the airframe and engine were simple. From the start, though punctuated by mild hiccups such as the departure of Fokker and distortions to the work-split caused by linking this to actual national purchases, everyone in Panavia has known exactly which company was responsible for which bit of the airframe. The general policy has been for all work to be done in the participating nations rather than at Panavia or some other central location. Possible disputes around the interfaces, such as the inlet ducts (German) leading to the engines (Turbo-Union) in the rear fuselage (British) were resolved right at the beginning, and instead of there being arguments the difficulty was usually to restrain the enthusiasm of all concerned. Not infrequently, in fact, more than one partner has checked and double-checked a vital borderline area, not because of distrust but to gain a fuller understanding of the problem. In earlier aircraft it has not been uncommon for design teams to make two mistakes which roughly cancelled out and thus gave an answer which looked right to the checkers; with three teams on the job this could hardly happen, and I think there are fewer mistakes in Tornado than in any comparable aircraft.

As the programme crystallised in early 1969 at a time when the biggest customer was Germany (in fact at that time the UK had not yet formally joined), Panavia was constituted under German law and the accounting unit was made the 1970 DM. On the other hand the standard language was made English, and an even odder fact is that in rationalising the use of SI (a 'pure' metric) units, such as pascals for pressure and newtons for thrust, it was the British who had to push their Continental partners! Technical standards were based on American MIL specs, and for a while this

caused alarm on many counts, one of the problems being that it was impractical to go to the fountain-head – probably someone in an office at Wright Field who would be politically unable to speak with Panavia – and clarify exact points of interpretation. In fact, standard were an amalgam of MIL with the highest common factors of all participating nations, plus a few national extras. It generated mountains of paperwork but led to a superb product (perhaps now we can rationalise and streamline the system for the next Panavia aeroplane). All contract procedures were absolutely tri-national and unified, adjusted where necessary to conform with national regulations. Especial attention was paid to the Panavia Design Standards Handbook, to the drawing standards, processes for computer-aided design, test procedures, QA (quality assurance) for suppliers, and true interchangeability of components secured via master reference tools. The procedures extend right through to logistic support to the aircraft now in service. Foreign evaluation teams say Panavia's overall operation is the best in the world, and it is one of those gigantic intangible assets that politicians have sometimes destroyed at the stroke of a pen.

More tangible are the hardware items that support a programme such as this. At many places in Europe, especially at Warton, Munich (and at the airfield at Manching 50 miles to the north) and Turin, scores of large and complex test rigs have explored every quirk of operation in all the Tornado's systems, night and day for many years. All three of the main airframe partners carried out extensive tunnel testing of models to explore aerodynamic drag, stability and control and many other factors. It has been calculated that, on a single-shift basis, over 40 tunnel-years of testing were accomplished in the early stages of the programme alone, using 30 major models. Even the relatively small test programme by Aeritalia had accounted for 147,000 test hours by the end of 1977, and the Italian partner then got down to the fatigue testing of production-standard wing flaps, spoilers and slats (which, of course, had not previously existed). Fatigue and endurance testing of one kind or another will continue throughout the whole life of the programme, certainly well beyond 2000.

In its early years the size of the programme in terms of numbers of aircraft was uncertain. The Germans at first said they wanted about 700, then in 1970 they announced a figure of '420 at the most' and in 1972 further reduced this to 322 – and finally amended to 324, as explained later. This and the departure of the Dutch reduced the total buy of the original partners from over 1,000 to a current figure of 809. Though the entire programme has from the start been subject to periodic checks by the three participating governments, from the start of 1973 it was possible to plan

with some assurance that over 800 aircraft would actually be built. This made it possible to fix levels of cost that came close to the original national limits, and to spend extremely large capital sums on test rigs, equipment and tooling without excessive commercial risk.

The point could be made yet again that it would have been possible to produce an aircraft broadly similar to the Tornado but simpler, with two-shaft engines, a large fixed wing and a reduced avionic fit and crew. Such an aircraft would probably have come out almost identical to today's F-18 Hornet. In one selected kind of mission it could have been made the equal of Tornado, but it is physically impossible to make it simultaneously equal in the other missions. Of course, it could be argued that a Hornet-type aircraft could have been developed quicker, and therefore (on grounds of inflation alone) delivered sooner and for less money. Whether this would have been a fair trade for the reduced capability is a moot point. What is beyond dispute is that Tornado exceeds the re-

quirements of the four initial customer services, and no other aircraft in existence comes near to it in this respect.

How many prototypes does one need in a programme of this type? In World War II the number of development aircraft in the biggest programmes, such as the Ju 88, ran into hundreds. In the 1950s Britain foolishly tried to build single aircraft in succession, so that an accident to the prototype brought everything to a stop. The US Air Force devised the Cook-Craigie Plan in which production tooling was made while the models were still in the wind-tunnels, but with rate of production initially kept low; then, as flight-test experience confirmed the absence of any real disaster in basic shape, the output was allowed to get into top gear, everyone accepting that large numbers of aircraft might need modifications later.

In this three-nation programme most of the decisions were studied with painstaking care. An airframe like Tornado cannot be 'handbuilt' and calls for numerically-controlled machining and hard tooling not greatly different from that used in production. At the same time, it would have been foolhardy to spend astronomic sums on the production tooling and wait until it was all in place, in completely new purpose-designed assembly shops at the three partners, before starting to make the first aircraft. What happened was that release of drawings and manufacturing of production tooling went ahead at full spate from 1972

Above: BT.001 was the first production aircraft, BT meaning British Trainer (though two-pilot is a more accurate description); it was photographed in the new Warton assembly hall near completion in December 1978./*BAe*

onwards. Both tasks gathered momentum, peaking at about the time the last of the original batch of prototypes took the air in early 1977.

In terms of timing, the main checkpoints were: 1 May 1969, start of Definition Phase; April 1970, completion of Definition Phase, but no decision by governments (for political reasons); July 1970, start of 'Pre-Development Phase'; 10 September 1971, statement by the three governments of Intention To Proceed after detailed review of requirements, costs and timescales; August 1972, full development contract awarded to Panavia; 15 March 1973, statement by the three governments following the fourth major review, announcing Intention To Proceed and authorising 'preparatory work for production' (officially called the Production Investment Phase, this permitted full-scale manufacture of tooling and buying of production materials and long-lead items); and 29 July 1976, Memorandum of Understanding by the three governments authorizing start of series production, plus order for the first 40 aircraft for inventory. Subsequently there have been further batch-orders, as described later, and these will continue.

With this kind of periodic-check programme it does not make a great deal of difference how many prototypes are ordered, provided nobody ever runs out of work. Originally, in 1969, 13 prototypes were ordered; then this was cut to seven, with standardisation of the two-seat airframe, and finally raised to nine. These have been followed by six pre-production aircraft, all built wholly (in theory at least) in production jigs, and increasingly indistinguishable from the production aircraft.

Overall the manufacturing programme thus looks as follows: Prototypes, nine (P.01-09); static-test airframe, one (10), pre-production, six (11-16) production, 805 (17 onwards) plus four refurbished pre-production aircraft, making 821 in all of which 809 are for inventory.

By aircraft sub-type: prototypes, 9; pre-production, 6; IDS version, 644; ADV, 165.

By recipient service: RAF, 220 Tornado GR1 (IDS) plus 165 F2 (ADV), total 385; Luftwaffe, 212 (all IDS); Marineflieger, 112 (all IDS); Aeronautica Militare Italiano, 100 (all IDS).

By operational function: combat duty, 671; trainers (full operational capability), 138.

By country of origin: prototypes, UK 4, Germany 3, Italy 2; static-test, UK 1; pre-production, UK 2, Germany 3, Italy 1; production, assembled in country of user service.

51

Flight Development

There are many ways of structuring a flight-test programme, and that for an aircraft as comprehensive as Tornado offered plenty of scope for choice – and for mistakes. To make things harder the whole programme had to be split into three, and even fed with inputs from other locations where the engine and certain weapon programmes were based. In some programmes, such as the USAF Light-Weight Fighters, the aim is to demonstrate the limits of flight performance as early as possible. With Tornado the aim was the different one of clearing a complete weapon system into operational service as early as possible. This much larger task had to be analysed in minute detail, planned as a number of successive interlocking steps, and divided laterally so that each of the three national flight-test centres would be able to work to a coherent and unbroken schedule which, as far as possible, was self-contained.

There are grounds for judging the Tornado flight-development task larger than in any other aircraft programme in history, because it involved a totally new airframe, engines and systems, with interfaces and weapon carriage to suit four major military customers. At the same time everything possible has been done to achieve standardisation, and it was particularly important to create a modern flight-test organisation with airborne telemetry of measured data direct on to magnetic tape or other stores on the ground, and – a vital point this – the best possible communications between the three centres and with industrial suppliers and government establishments. The existence of Panavia and NAMMA as single three-nation organisations was a significant help in simplifying communications, but the inherent multiplicity of com-

Right: XT272, one of the extremely valuable Buccaneers used by the CDMT to ensure that the main avionics matured ahead of the aircraft./*BAe*

munications links did make this a more difficult programme to manage than ones where there is one prime
contractor, one test centre and one customer.

Aircraft used in the flight-development programme
are listed in an Appendix. In the previous chapter it
was explained how, whereas production Tornados are
assembled in the country of use, the first 16 were
assigned to particular centres: four prototypes, the
static-test airframe and two pre-production at Warton,
three prototypes and three pre-production at
Manching, and two prototypes and one pre-production
at Caselle. Warton, on the north shore of the river
Ribble west of Preston in Lancashire, is the airfield
and engineering centre of what used to be BAC
Military Aircraft Division and is now the Warton
Division of British Aerospace Aircraft Group.
Manching is about 50 miles north of Munich (site of
Panavia's headquarters and the MBB plant at
Ottobrunn), beside the Autobahn and near the city of
Ingolstadt and the river Danube. Caselle is about 10
miles north of Turin and is the city's airport as well as
the chief centre of Aeritalia's Combat Aircraft Group.

All three had previously been the site of major
flight-test programmes involving supersonic combat
aircraft, but never anything approaching the scale of
this programme. The telemetry systems were largely
new in European experience, and in each case
represent an important national capital asset that will
extend beyond Tornado into the next century. Further
new installations include simulators to give
preliminary training to the test pilots as well as solving
problems for the engineers. Simulation today plays a

Above: This close formation shot of P.02 in cruise configuration
shows the neat nozzles clearly./*BAe*

Above right: Aircraft 08 was the second of the two-pilot Tornados,
and the first of this species to be equipped for blind navigation and
weapon-aiming./*BAe*

Right: No 13 returns to Manching from doppler-monitored inertial
tests, ground crew getting at the handy avionics even before the
steps arrive./*MBB*

central role in all advanced aircraft programmes right
from the time that the customer begins to draw up his
preliminary specifications. (As these words are written,
the various simulators in Panavia's three main centres
have obviously been busy, off and on, for several years
trying to help the three nations find the next-generation
small 'fighter'; it would be a tragedy if the aim of a
common aircraft were this time to prove elusive.) By
early 1973 the three Panavia companies working on
the airframe had each selected two test pilots, who at
once began studying the detailed engineering of the
Tornado and training on simulators.

Basic communication between the three centres by
telephone and Telex was naturally backed up by
personal visits. In a programme of this size and importance it is sensible to use one's own jets, and these included a 125, Hansa Jet and often a One-Eleven from
the Weybridge/Bristol Division to carry a whole team

of 30 engineers and stacks of drawings or hardware. The distance from Warton to Manching, about an hour and a half by jet, is enough to make it a long day; engineers at either centre have to be stirring by about 5am, for a 7am take-off. On most days a 125 and Hansa Jet pass each other, and pass again in the evening. Often the weather has been atrocious. Sadly, MBB lost a delegation of engineers on 29 June 1972 when a Hansa Jet crashed on take-off from Squires Gate (Blackpool), used instead of Warton because of the need to clear Customs. Travel accounted for 3.3 per cent of the total Tornado development cost; at the same time, spending a lot of time in the air is no bad thing for aircraft designers.

In the early 1970s, when the flight-development programme was planned in great detail, broad-brush decisions were taken that represented the best compromises between giving each company a coherent self-contained programme, fitting in with the emergence of the prototypes, making sensible progress, and avoiding duplication. It was decided that the first aircraft should fly at Manching, with MBB thus inevitably responsible for the first general handling and performance measurement. But the German partner's main assignment concerned the most complex area of all: integration of the avionics and flight-control systems, so aircraft 04, the first with the integrated avionics system, was possibly the most important of all nine prototypes. The second aircraft was arranged to fly in England, and BAC Warton was given primary responsibility for what are the basic parts of any flight-

test programme; exploring the flight envelope with the aircraft clean, flight loads on the structure, propulsion, stalling, spinning and so forth. The British partner was also given the dual two-pilot programme (so the first of these was assembled at Warton) and, so that its immense electronics expertise should be fully utilised, was also charged with clearing the avionics for the RAF Tornado GR1 (especially where they are non-standard) along with any peculiarly British weapon fits. Aeritalia was assigned the main responsibility for flight with external stores.

Obviously such a scheme has to have some areas of overlap. For example, all three partners did their own investigations into general handling and performance, and, by the very nature of the aircraft, into avionics. Though MBB was recognised as chief avionics integrator, with specific responsibility for domestic systems such as autopilot, flight system, navigation, landing aids and communications, it was obviously desirable for each partner to work closely through NAMMA with its own customer air force to make certain that the latter was happy with its own Tornados. Though the basic avionics just mentioned are standard for all versions, there are many differences in detail, and larger differences in operational equipment as explained later.

Flight development began with the first flight of an early prototype RB.199 under the Vulcan in April 1973. It was planned to complete a programme totalling 320 hours, using successive engines in this pod, within 18 months. Unfortunately, the Vulcan suffered unexpected structural and electrical trouble which greatly reduced the achieved flying rate. This was serious, because in 1974-77 the engine was indisputably the pacing item in the Tornado flight programme, and intensive flying in the Vulcan would have assisted its swifter maturity. In 1974 a flight-standard

RB.199-01 was substituted and behaviour of the whole installation explored at various throttle settings during gun firing trials. Early flying of this test bed did at least confirm the narrow surge margins, the problems with the MECU (main-engine control unit) and oil starvation, and also the ability to shed blades without the crew being aware of it. Far from being a chapter of disasters, the early history of the engine was actually encouraging, for this extremely advanced and compact engine demonstrated potential at least as good as prediction and combined this with superb handling.

During the early period, when all the test pilots could do was fly the simulators, and handle the engine on the test-bed or in the Vulcan, an official request was made to the US Department of Defense to permit nominated Panavia test pilots to fly the F-111, their time being fully paid for. Whenever there is a whiff of commercial competition affecting the United States the Western Alliance takes a back seat, and this request was refused. Even at this early stage I noticed studied efforts by numerous Americans to try to 'knock' the MRCA, as it was then called. Without naming the individuals, I recall three choice quotes: 'It makes no sense to us' (Northrop, Beverly Hills, 1973); 'You know the definition of a camel – a horse designed by a committee?' (McDonnell Douglas, Paris, 1973); and 'We will be surprised if it ever gets into production' (Department of Defense, 1973). Combined with the best efforts of Dassault-Breguet, the Americans initially did all they could to ensure that the media never lacked ammunition with which to hit the programme. They need not have bothered; once MRCA had got into the media as an Aunt Sally, to replace Concorde, the knocking was a self-generating process. Even as I write, well into 1979, a BBC TV documentary on aviation had only two things to say about Tornado; it is 'not an outstanding aircraft' and 'the only outstanding thing about it is its cost'.

The one thing the media seldom bothered to do with Tornado was speak to the men who flew it. There was naturally intense competition to make the first flight, and had he chosen to do so not many would have argued against R.P. 'Bee' Beamont; but the veteran test pilot had been appointed Panavia Director of Flight Operations and did not get his hands on Tornado until August 1975. Eventually a compromise was struck: P.01 would fly at Manching, but in the hands of a British pilot. To preserve MBB morale the backseater would be a German.

The aircraft was structurally complete in the autumn of 1973, and on 12 November was shrouded in fabric – ostensibly to preserve security of the inlets and other sensitive features – and trucked from Ottobrunn to Manching. The press release said it would then have ground-running engines installed, complete taxying trials and then, early next year make

its first flight. In fact various delays, among them flight-clearance of the RB.199-01 engine, delayed the start of flight testing by six months. The time was not wholly lost, because throughout the first half of 1974 P.01 was continually updated to ever-higher technical standard which had mainly been planned in 1973 but had originally been intended to be incorporated as post-flight modifications. At the same time 01 was still a relatively basic aircraft, packed with instrumentation in place of operational avionics.

It was on 14 August 1974 that Paul Millett, then styled BAC Military Aircraft Division Chief Test Pilot and Project Pilot MRCA, settled into the front cockpit (which he had done many times before on various checks and 'dry runs'), and his opposite number at MBB, Nils Meister, into the back. In dull and overcast weather they took-off with wings at 26°, partial flap and full afterburner. Rotating, they unstuck cleanly and climbed away at an angle which became progressively steeper in order to stay inside the gear-down limit at the light weight of some 39,000lb. Afterburner was gradually reduced until, with a Luftwaffe TF-104G watching from one side and a G91T from the other, the new bird settled into cruise at 10,000ft, still in take-off configuration. Millett checked behaviour in a simulated approach, in case a quick return was necessary; then he cleaned 01 up and checked handling in turns at successively higher speeds to 300kts. The full flight system with electrical signalling, autopilot and CSAS was operative throughout. After explorations in the vertical plane and various functional tests, Millett opened up the engines back into afterburner, in case he had to make an unplanned go-around at the last moment. Back at Manching the flaps were again lowered to the take-off setting, and the gear extended. Millett deliberately flew a missed approach, and landed off the second. Landing speed was some 20kts higher than optimum for the weight, from the addition of the normal first-flight safety increment plus use of take-off flap only. Reversers were used as well as jabs of wheel brake.

Everything had gone perfectly. The 30-minute flight had covered every one of the planned test points, and there was neither a system failure nor a spurious fault-indication. No adjustment of any kind was needed after landing, though several days were then spent on the ground in a planned programme of other work. The weather then clamped, delaying the second flight and ultimately losing 11 days in the first winter at Manching. Millett and Meister finally made a 50-minute second flight a week after the first, checking wing sweeps to 45°, single-engine flight (including simulated approach and overshoot), effect of airbrakes, and flight control with certain failure-modes simulated. Again the aircraft landed fully serviceable. For the third flight, on 29 August, the two test pilots

changed places. Just as swinging the wings had been demonstrated one flight earlier than planned, so was the changing of places, the MBB pilot not having been scheduled to take over until Flight 4. On the third mission Meister explored handling with the wings at all angles to 68°, with no trouble at all. Speed built up during the process to Mach 1.15.

Despite the bad weather and other causes for delay, the start of MRCA flying had been as encouraging as that of the engine. Basically, the aircraft was a delight to fly – not just good, but better than any aircraft the test pilots had ever known, and in all configurations and conditions. Serviceability had proved excellent, leading to the belief that the planned rate of eight hours per aircraft per month would comfortably be achieved. No less important was the good behaviour of the extremely complete airborne instrumentation and ground data-processing, and the telemetry that linked them together. As for measurements of such parameters as drag and fuel flow, these were degraded in value by the as-yet unrepresentative standard of engine; but general compatibility with predicted performance was described officially as 'very good indeed'.

While aircraft 01 continued its valuable work, development of the Tornado's gun was assisted by a Lightning F2A leased by the MoD to IKWA-Mauser on behalf of Panavia. Based at Warton and maintained and flown by BAC staff, it was tasked with proving the

MK27 in the air, under all combinations of IAS and g. There was little difficulty in fitting the new gun on the left side of the belly tank, previously occupied by a 30mm Aden. Air firing with live ammunition took place at West Freugh and Eskmeals in southern Scotland, and raised few problems. This completely new gun, whose second application is in the Luftwaffe light attack version of the Alpha Jet, was one of the first major Tornado items to be cleared for production. The Vulcan engine test-bed was used to check engine behaviour and gas-ingestion during gun firing under various flight conditions. When firing began from Tornado 06 it was mainly a job of confirming these results.

While 01 was still the only Tornado flying it was found that the flight-control system was extremely sensitive. As explained in the next chapter, in the normal mode the system is a computerised manoeuvre-demand system, and in such a system the demand – sensed by electric potentiometers on the pilot's inputs – sometimes tends to drive the control surface(s) slightly too far and too fast until the pilot restores the null position. This is fine for air combat, but from the first flight the very low break-out force (force needed to move the controls from the neutral position) and transient overcontrol response naturally resulted in suggestions from the test pilots. At first the extreme sensitivity was thought to affect mainly roll and yaw; and 'notchiness' in roll — tending to prevent smooth infinitely-varying rate of roll according to stick position — was also investigated.

The pilot can set any flight-control mode he wishes, and from the second flight the testing investigated failed electrical signal channels resulting, first, in direct-link control (without the computerised CSAS) and ultimately, after a succession of failures, in direct mechanical control to the tailerons only, still amply sufficient to fly the aircraft. These extreme degraded modes were described by Meister as 'far better than predictions or requirements', and all that was needed was a small mechanical redesign to reduce friction in the mechanically signalled mode. More significant was the superb and wholly reliable performance of the full system, so that from quite early in the programme there was a prospect of eliminating the manual back-up system. This had not been decided in the spring of 1979, but it would make the aircraft lighter, simpler and cheaper.

Increasingly aircraft 01 became unrepresentative of the production Tornado and so, while later prototypes took over the measurement of aerodynamic factors such as drag and performance, 01 concentrated on engine development. It did most of the proving of the reverser installation, previously developed on engine test-beds, and perfected directional stability on the runway at full reverse thrust with modified buckets which attach the airflow to the fin to keep the rudder effective. It had been planned to re-engine 01 with the full-thrust -04 engines in mid-1977, but these took longer to develop and did not get into the air in 01 until March 1978. These were the first full-thrust engines to fly. In 1979 aircraft 01, still in its original colour scheme, was busy with various engine, CSAS and other investigations.

Aircraft 02, assembled in England and at first painted red and white like 01, can fairly be regarded as the workhorse of the prototype fleet, and has certainly flown the most hours. Its main tasks have been to explore the flight envelope, and carry out stalling, spinning and both the low-speed and extremely high-speed investigations. It was the first Tornado with fully variable engine inlets, enabling it to take all that the engines could give at all Mach numbers. In its investigations into the upper end of the speed spectrum 02 made a level run in early May 1977 which was terminated by the pilot as the Mach number was still climbing beyond 1.93. This was achieved on -03 engines, and there was a slight overtemperature problem in the reheat (afterburner) system which tem-

porarily precluded further investigation. It was clear, however, that the production aircraft would be one of the fastest combat aircraft, with clean altitude performance easily exceeding Mach 2. (As described later, the ADV fighter is even faster.)

More important, Tornado is probably the fastest aircraft in the world at tree-top height. Again still fitted with -03 engines, aircraft 02 demonstrated indicated airspeeds just in excess of 800kts (921mph). Only a few combat aircraft are permitted to reach 750kts, and most are red-lined — for structural, thermal or other reasons — at 700kts or below. Such speeds at low level are extremely tough on any aircraft, and certainly no fixed-sweep aircraft could be operated effectively under such conditions; the crew discomfort would be intolerable, and fatigue life of the primary structure consumed very rapidly. In 1979 Tornados had flown several hours at indicated airspeeds around the 800-knot level, representing about Mach 1.3 at typical northern-Europe temperatures. I have not heard of a severe bird-strike, and can only presume that if in dire emergency the crew had to eject, the seat would function correctly at such a speed, which is way beyond the normal upper limit for a Mk 10 seat of 630kts (fully adequate for other aircraft).

Much of 02's flying has been at low speeds at extremely high angles of attack. Swing-wing aircraft in the maximum-sweep configuration can fly at angles of attack far beyond the stalling limits for fixed-wing aircraft. Probably Tornado could reach angles beyond 60°, and values exceeding 30° were demonstrated by 02 even with the wings unswept, which is unusual. In spring 1977 this aircraft was fitted with a gantry on the rear fuselage housing a spin-recovery parachute. It was also given a hydrazine-fuelled MEPU (monofuel emergency power unit). I had been surprised at the lack of any means of driving the hydraulics, vital in order to fly the aeroplane, following loss of both engines; thus, if you ran out of fuel when within gliding distance of the runway, you still had to eject. We had been through all this with the Jaguar, one of which was lost due to 'finger trouble' by a French pilot; the answer on this aircraft was to provide an electrically driven pump which cuts in automatically following double engine failure. The Harrier, in contrast, has a ram-air windmill. The Tornado has nothing, because that was what the customers specified. Stalling and spinning was thought to pose a reasonable risk of double flame-out, which in the aircraft as originally designed could mean ejection. So Sundstrand in the United States, whose customers are more interested in emergency supplies, sold Panavia the F-15 type MEPU, with which the Warton pilots have safely explored stalls and spins. Even after spin entries at angles of attack well beyond 30° there were no problems, and recovery proved to be straightforward.

According to Beamont one of the acid tests of the handling of a modern combat aircraft is how easily the pilot can take fuel from a tanker. Nothing could more eloquently testify to Tornado's beautiful handling than the fact that the entire aerial refuelling programme was cleared virtually in one flight, made by 02 back in July 1975. The tanker was a Victor K2, XL158 of No 57 Squadron, and film records taken from the tanker and a chase Canberra confirmed the uncanny rock-steadiness of the Tornado throughout the operation. Though the pilot had ample positive control in the fore/aft direction with throttles and airbrakes, the air-craft rode so smoothly that for long periods the film record seemed to have been arrested, but for a single clue: the winking anti-collision light. Clearing inflight refuelling enabled the flying rate to go up considerably by scheduling a tanker on many of the test flights, thus leading to sorties normally running to several hours and resulting in whole volumes of data, with major test programmes completed between each take-off and touchdown.

Another important early task of 02 was to clear carriage of some of the largest external stores, and in-vestigate flutter modes with them in place. The first to fly were the 330Imp gal (1,500litre) tanks on the inner swivelling wing pylons. All four pylons on the outer wing naturally have to be kept aligned with the air-stream at all wing angles, and so are mounted on pivots and rotated by mechanical linkage inside the wing. These big tanks caused no trouble at all; in fact

Above: Flight refuelling was virtually cleared in a single sortie; here a Canadian pilot takes fuel rather close (almost at boom distance) behind a No 57 Squadron Victor K2./*BAe*

Above right: Representative load for 06 in 1977 was eight BL.755 cluster bombs, two 1,500-litre tanks and two MSDS Ajax advanced ECM pods./*BAe*

the BAC test pilots argued among themselves whether the aircraft was even smoother with them on! Actual flight-test data did show a reduction in buffet at high g with the wings at maximum sweep, but I think in other modes the supposed 'extra smoothness' must be in the mind. The tank pylons are slightly deeper than those for weapons or ECM in order for the tank tails to clear the tailerons at full control deflection with the wing at 68° (another example of 'belt and braces' because at the speeds associated with 68° the taileron angles would be extremely small). It was found later in the programme that, with full tanks, aeroelastic deflection of the wing and taileron could result in the two almost coming together at 68° sweep, and the cure was to shave a little off the outer leading edge of the taileron by increasing the sweep, resulting in a kink.

Aircraft 03, the second assembled at Warton and flown in August 1975, was the first dual two-pilot version. Camouflaged from the start, and fitted with a radome (but no radar), it was the chief high-incidence

vehicle used for stalls and spins. It was also used for the direct measurement of air loads in flight, a technique impossible until the 1960s but one which virtually removes the problem caused by the unreliability of measurements with models in tunnels. Early in its career tests were flown at very close to the stall, and the pronounced contrast between the full CSAS system and the direct link with CSAS switched off was verified. Panavia later followed Grumman's example in recommending automatic limitation of pilot authority at very high angles of attack as a means of making a stall/spin accident impossible (something that would have saved many lives in Phantoms).

One of the few serious incidents in the flight-development programme befell P.03 on 4 October 1976. Warton is one of Europe's wetter places, and the aircraft made a landing on that date in torrential rain on a runway covered in varying thicknesses of standing water. Pilot Ferguson was unable to stop the aircraft sliding diagonally off the runway, striking the grass verge and coming to rest on the nosewheel, rear fuselage and wingtip. The result was: stiffening of the main-leg mounting brackets; revision of reverser geometry to improve flow over the rudder and preserve symmetric thrust; and introduction of nosewheel steering augmentation for such extraordinary conditions. So this was actually a useful accident, and while 03 was under repair it was put in the Warton static-test rig for eight weeks for a complete programme of structural load calibration.

Subsequently 03 demonstrated its return to health by carrying out the extreme-weight trials. At the start of 1978 it took off at 56,000lb, much heavier than most previous flying, and two weeks later pushed up to 58,400. Still with -03 engines, it demonstrated that the pilot had nothing to worry about, and in fact could apply full taileron for maximum rate of roll even at maximum weight with the limiting underwing load.

As already mentioned, aircraft 04 has probably been the most important of all nine prototypes, because it introduced the flight development of the avionics. But in fact major elements of these systems had previously begun flying in the two valuable CDMT Buccaneers based on the hack aircraft hangar at Warton from November 1974. Though completely rebuilt by Marshalls of Cambridge as the CDMT 'Stage 3' rigs to fly all the larger items in the Tornado avionic systems, the conversion did not extend to a digital flight-control system. Thus these otherwise superb trials platforms are unable to simulate Tornado's automated terrain-following and weapon-delivery, with the autopilot slaved to the TFR radar or other sensors. In most other respects they have few limitations, and as this was written, in early 1979, had flown over 600 hours in the programme, most of it on arduous missions at high speed and low level. One could add that the Buccaneer, tough old bird that it is, is no picnic in rough air at full throttle, while the molly-coddled Tornado pilot rides in the utmost smoothness with wings at 68° wondering why the

Above: Tornado 04 originally had serial D-9592 on the tailerons, but is seen here after repainting in MFG livery; MFG aircraft are not specially marinised because the basic standard of corrosion protection is so high. /*MBB*

other chap is complaining. So equipment that works reliably in the Buccaneer ought to work in Tornado.

Despite the back-up provided by the Buccaneers, Tornado 04 was nevertheless a vital aircraft. It alone amassed virtually all the avionics data needed for the production go-ahead decision in one series of 12 flights in 1975-76. It was the first aircraft to integrate the standard TI forward radar, TFR, doppler and other navigation and weapon-aiming systems, through the digital autopilot and flight-control system, to fly the aircraft automatically. A vast amount of effort was needed to make the whole mass of integrated equipment work properly. From late 1975 aircraft 04 was regularly going out with a formidable list of tasks, ranging from precise checking of the accuracy of the inertial navigation (by kine-theodolite checks of its actual position at the end of the long flight, and comparison with the INS readout at that instant) to such matters as finding hiccups in the software, improving the HUD symbology and perfecting the brightness and

uniformity of the tabular displays. The most complex items, the central and air-data computers, gave surprisingly little trouble. By 1977 this Tornado was often engaged in weapon trials, and was the first to fly the grotesque MW-1 anti-armour installation.

Italy's first Tornado, P.05, was the only prototype to have a really unlucky early history. Its first flight was delayed some five months by unavailability of suitable engines, and did not take place until December 1975. In high-visibility white/red, it nevertheless had proper national markings and a radome, unlike 01 and 02, and thus looked a particularly attractive machine. Tasked with flutter and load measurement, it had completed a bare six flights when, in January 1976, it was so severely damaged as to make repair doubtful. Announced as a 'heavy landing' at Caselle, it was more accurately called a crash, caused primarily by the sensitivity of the pitch channel. The nose hit the ground with such force that major structural damage ensued. It was sheer luck this took place at Caselle, as this made repair worthwhile, but 05 was not back in the sky until March 1978. This inevitably left a hole in the programme, but thanks to the prior contingency plans 02 was able to take over 05's flutter work, with instrumentation already installed. It is in such emergencies that the establishment of three compatible

Above left: MBB's chief test pilot, 'Fred' Rammensee (right) congratulates Fritz Soos, first Government test pilot to fly Tornado, on 26 November 1975./*MBB*

Above: Paul Millett, Warton manager of flight operations (and only pilot so far to make three Tornado 'first flights') seen (right) on 8 September 1977 with the UK Controller of Aircraft, Air Chief Marshal Sir Douglas Lowe./*BAe*

Left: David Eagles, Warton divisional chief test pilot./*BAe*

flight-test centres really paid off. The rebuilt 05 has a new forward fuselage and wears AMI camouflage.

Aircraft 06, assembled at Warton, introduced a new rear fuselage of slightly slimmer profile. Almost the only aerodynamic problem encountered in the entire programme was a tendency to snake at about Mach 0.9. Warton handled most of this investigation, trying a large number of often seemingly trivial changes to the profiles of the spine and rear fuselage. Unlike the F-111 there was never a drag problem; it was just that the boundary layer was breaking away at the base of the fin, causing mild directional instability at high subsonic speed. With 06 the revised profile and longer sharp-lipped fairing under the rudder cured the problem. Later the trailing edge of the rudder and fairing

were made to form a straight line right down to the nozzles, without altering the proven geometry of the reversers.

The main task of 06 was armament development. In early 1976 it completed a crucial series of tests in which stores were released for the first time. One cannot help commenting on the way in which the availability of more aircraft and more flight-cleared engines allowed flying rate to increase, and recover most of the ground lost in the early years. February 1976 saw 33 flights, a record, but in March 1976 the total was 67. No fewer than 14 of these were by 06, which by the end of the month had completed the provision of all data needed on stores-separation for the production go-ahead. Most of the stores were 1,500 litre tanks and dummy 1,000lb bombs. Once this was out of the way 06 was re-equipped and instrumented for gun-firing trials, at first at the Warton butts and then, from April 1978, under all flight conditions. As in the stores-separation tests, no problems were encountered. Nobody wants problems, but the lack of them in almost all parts of the Tornado seemed at times uncanny.

By aircraft 07 the Tornado was beginning to mature, and prototypes were emerging with changes resulting from flight test. I had a personal feeling that 07, the second avionics aircraft and third assembled at Manching, was the first that could pass as a production Tornado to the visitor walking round it (though the expert might have known better!). As far as possible its standard duplicated 04 so that each could backup the other, but in fact 07 introduced a near-production autopilot and spent a full year on intensive low flying on specially designated routes, most of them across the Black Forest, proving the most vital of all subsystems: that linking the TFR, radar altimeters, flight controls, CSAS, HUD and weapon-aiming. Everything was fine, apart from a sudden

Above: Aircraft 12 about to depart, testing functioning of spoilers and reversers before a sortie at A&AEE Boscombe Down./*BAe*

Above right: ZA319, the first of 805 production Tornados in the initial programme for inventory service, made an 87-minute flight from Warton on 10 July 1979. Known in Panavia shorthand as BT.001 (first British trainer) it is seen in the hands of Dave Eagles and Ray Woollett./*BAe*

autopilot runaway (a fault condition tending to ask the aircraft to make an undesired violent manoeuvre) in August 1977. This caused a flurry of activity and will not happen again.

Aircraft 08, from Warton, was the first specifically tasked with weapon aiming. But it was also a dual two-pilot machine, and as well as completing clearance of that version became the first Tornado to welcome aboard a senior officer from a customer air force. The occasion was a visit to Warton by Gen Ciarlo, Chief of Staff of the Aeronautica Militare Italiano. With Aeritalia's Chief Test Pilot in the front cockpit, the general took-off from the British centre and for the next 40 minutes concentrated on seeing what the tri-national Tornado could do, mostly at tree-top height among the rugged Pennines. After this period had elapsed, test pilot Trevisan complained 'I haven't had my hands on the stick yet!' This underlines the remarkable way in which the programme allows two people whom some Britishers might call 'foreign' to wring out a British Tornado over Britain. It also demonstrates the superb qualities of the aircraft – and equally of the Italian Chief of Staff.

P.09, flown at Caselle on the same day as Germany's P.11, spent most of its first year in Sicily on flutter tests with the three most critical national stores

configurations, including stores-separation tests. Because of the environment, hot-weather trials were run in parallel, and despite being far from home at a base lacking special Tornado equipment, 09 was almost continually serviceable and kept up a high flying rate. Data were recorded on tapes at a mobile ground terminal, which were thereafter flown to Caselle for analysis. Then followed several months at Decimomannu, Sardinia, on weapon firing. Trevisan commented: 'Though the airspace was crowded with aircraft from NATO air forces there was never any problem ... We even flew three times a day.' Among missiles launched by 09 in July 1978 was Kormoran, to be carried by Tornados of the Marineflieger.

P.11, the first German-assembled two-pilot aircraft, was to have gone quickly to the Federal German OTC (Official Test Centre) at Manching for final contractual performance tests. Instead it happened to be the first aircraft with a production-standard fillet along the junction between the rear fuselage and vertical tail, and it was kept back by Panavia for measurement of total aircraft drag. While these measures were being made it was flown by a galaxy of service chiefs; at the same time British commanders and the Minister of Defence flew 03 and 08.

P.12, assembled at Warton, was the first Tornado to be delivered. In tri-national markings but with a British serial number, it flew from Warton to the A&AEE at Boscombe Down on 3 February 1978. Boscombe had assembled a tri-national team from the four customer air forces who pounced on the new aircraft and have flown it hard even since. In early 1979 it still had -03 engines, and the airframe was not to production standard, but it has done more than any other Tornado to knock the few rough edges off the avionics, make sure the aircraft can do its job with live weapons and keep up an intensive flying rate, whilst simultaneously checking out future Tornado instructors.

The final four pre-production aircraft were very close to production standard. P.13 (German) introduced the kinked taileron leading edge. P.14 (Italian) introduced production wings. P.15 (British) at last flew the final production-standard rear fuselage and wet fin. P.16 (German) brought in the production front fuselage from Warton, and was the first aircraft assembled on the MBB assembly line at Manching. Previously MBB had assembled at Ottobrunn and, with wings at 68° and vertical tail packed separately, trucked Tornados by road to Manching. From No 16, aircraft have been assembled at Manching in a way reminiscent of a car factory, with a powered assembly line and many other advanced features, with all power services routed under the floor to meet the severe German rules on industrial noise. As this is written, the first production machine, BT.001, has just come off the line on 5 June 1979 at another completely new facility, at British Aerospace, Warton. GT.001 was rolled out at the new Manching factory the following day.

Tornado flight development, for various purposes, will continue for many years. So far it has been probably the most successful in military-aircraft history. Despite the vast breadth of tasks undertaken in three countries, the IDS version has been cleared to higher standards than those guaranteed to the origianl four customers, with greater fuel and weapons loads, better navigation and weapon-delivery accuracy and several other achievements beyond prediction. And this has been done without the loss of a single aircraft or injury to a crew-member. Can any other modern combat-aircraft programme claim as much?

[On the very day I wrote this, 12 June 1979, Tornado 08 disappeared, with no radio message, while flying at low level in mist over the Irish Sea. Pilot was the brilliant project pilot Russ Pengelly; navigator Sqn Ldr John Gray from A&AEE.]

How it Works

A book on a modern lightplane, or an older military aircraft, might not need a chapter with such a title. A book of this kind does not concern itself with 'principles of flight', or the insides of gas turbines or hydraulic systems, but it is hardly possible to write a book on the Tornado without at least superficially explaining how it does its job. As is by now obvious, the jobs of the Tornado are varied. The simplest is pilot type-conversion and weapon training in good weather. Then comes day attack on surface targets previously seen by the crew (in the jargon of the trade, 'acquired by eye'). More difficult are the two most important kinds of mission: blind first-pass attack on surface targets, on land or sea, and all-weather interception and air superiority combat.

The air-to-air missions, which are central to the Tornado ADV featured in the next chapter, call for specific operating modes of the main radar (air-to-air search, lock-on and angle tracking, followed by ranging for the weapons) and special weapons such as air-to-air missiles and the two guns in the rapid-fire mode. But the main part of this chapter explains the avionics and weapons for surface attack, because it is these that enable the Tornado to fly safely in all weathers, navigate with precision and hit even the most difficult target accurately. In passing, I cannot resist again commenting on the attitude of the media. Writers and broadcasters used to regard Tornado as the ultimate villainous example of technology gone mad at the taxpayer's expense; according to a national daily 'It is packed with costly "black box" toys to please the air marshals', while a TV feature tells the world 'It is a plane built to excite the technologists'. This nonsensical feeling arose in 1964 during the

Right: Tornado 07, here flying completely clean, greatly extended the early avionics testing of 04 and finally proved the complete integrated system./*MBB*

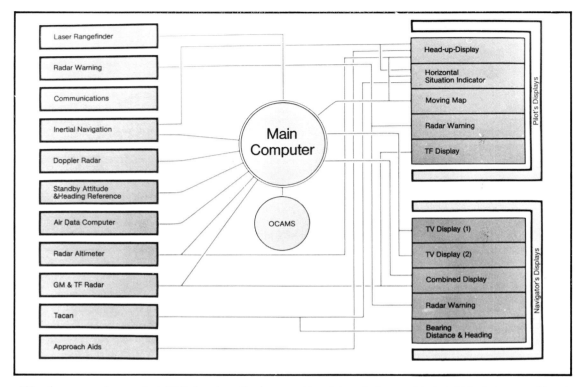

Laser Rangefinder

Radar Warning

Communications

Inertial Navigation

Doppler Radar

Standby Attitude & Heading Reference

Air Data Computer

Radar Altimeter

GM & TF Radar

Tacan

Approach Aids

Main Computer

OCAMS

Pilot's Displays

Head-up-Display

Horizontal Situation Indicator

Moving Map

Radar Warning

TF Display

Navigator's Displays

TV Display (1)

TV Display (2)

Combined Display

Radar Warning

Bearing Distance & Heading

vilification campaign against TSR.2, when the incoming government deliberately fostered the belief that that aircraft was horrifically and needlessly expensive because of its complex avionics. Anyone who uses his brain for three consecutive seconds will perhaps see that in an environment of extreme financial stringency money is unlikely to be wasted, and that more avionics may well mean fewer aircraft. A further three seconds of applied reasoning may lead to the conclusion that to leave out the '"black box" toys' would not really save money. All it would achieve would be to reduce Tornado to the same status as most other aircraft in Western air forces, which are unable to fly the missions in the kind of weather when they are most likely to be needed.

The best way to see how the avionic system works is with a diagram, but it is still no easy task to break it down into its essentials. This is partly because the avionics do not stop at those shown in the diagram but continue, via the autopilot and flight director, into the CSAS (command stability augmentation system) and both primary and secondary flight-control systems. As depicted, the avionics do no more than present visual information to the pilot and navigator. In reality they can take over and fly the aircraft – to drop a bomb automatically on a target, intercept a hostile aircraft, avoid a tall tree or make a blind automatic landing.

Above: Schematic diagram of the basic IDS avionic system./*Panavia*

Above right: Simplified block diagram of the Texas Instruments IDS radar, with plate aerial on the right and aircraft interfaces on the left./*Panavia*

These links between the avionics sensors and the Tornado's tailerons, spoilers and rudder should not be forgotten.

One thing that is obvious is that most information is routed through the main nav/attack computer. This acts as a general post office; it also stores information for use when needed, processes it in microseconds, and feeds it to different places. As Tornado is a modern aircraft, all information is digital. This means it is supplied, processed and fed in the form of rapid sequences of very small electrical pulses, or 'bits'. Millions circulate inside Tornado, and large numbers reside in its computer memory even when it is parked on the flight-line. Digital data are more accurate than the old analog kind, and among other advantages are less susceptible to electrical interference, either from the masses of electrics and emissions on board

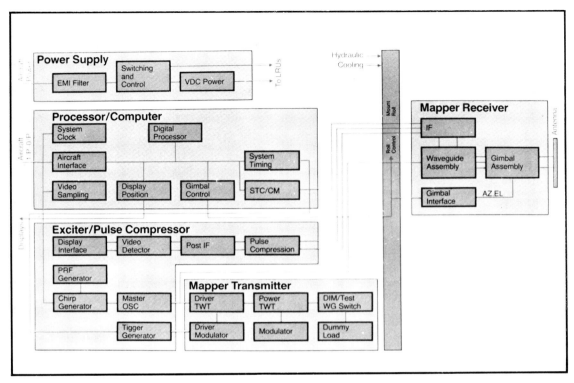

Power Supply
- EMI Filter
- Switching and Control
- VDC Power
- To LRUs

Hydraulic Cooling

Mount Roll

Roll Control

Mapper Receiver
- IF
- Waveguide Assembly
- Gimbal Assembly
- Gimbal Interface
- AZ EL
- Antenna

Processor/Computer
- System Clock
- Digital Processor
- Aircraft Interface
- System Timing
- Video Sampling
- Display Position
- Gimbal Control
- STC/CM

Exciter/Pulse Compressor
- Display Interface
- Video Detector
- Post IF
- Pulse Compression
- PRF Generator
- Chirp Generator
- Master OSC
- Tigger Generator

Mapper Transmitter
- Driver TWT
- Power TWT
- DIM/Test WG Switch
- Driver Modulator
- Modulator
- Dummy Load

Tornado or from deliberate interference by the enemy. Digital data are also compatible with modern solid-state microelectronics, which save weight and bulk, and reduce current consumption and heat to be dissipated.

It is this provision of great data-processing power, in fast and versatile digital computers, that has done more than anything else to revolutionise the modern tactical aircraft. A close second is the provision of sensors, which are devices for 'seeing', measuring or in some other way reacting to something outside the aircraft. Two combat aircraft may look alike, and seem to fly alike, but their value to an air force – especially in a highly sophisticated hostile environment in extremely bad weather – is determined almost totally by their sensors and computing power. Tornado is officially said to 'set new standards in this field'.

In the rest of this chapter I will outline the sensors first, then describe the displays that impart the information to the two crew, and finally add brief details of the further interface with the flight-control system. The point may not be obvious that there are at least three distinct facets to a typical IDS mission. One is the flying of the aircraft as an end in itself, and as this almost certainly means very low flying for at least part of the trip the TFR (terrain-following radar) and HUD (head-up display) are needed for this alone, and so are the landing aids needed for a safe recovery at the end of the mission. The second is navigation, so that the aircraft can fly the exact route the crew wish it to. The third is to detect or identify targets and obtain information (photographs or other data) or launch weapons against them. With some psychological effort, it would be possible safely to fly a Tornado using very few sensors other than the pitot/static system, and with the computer and displays switched off. Thus, anyone who can fly a simple jet could fly a Tornado, and probably find it easier; but a real mission is carefully planned beforehand and makes use of almost every black box on board.

Largest and in some respects most important sensor is the radar. This really comprises two radars, both made by Texas Instruments; the GM (ground-mapping) radar and the TFR (terrain-following radar). The installation occupies the whole nose of the aircraft and is optimised for air-to-ground use, though with full air-to-air facilities available. Earlier it was suggested that the TI radar was chosen because it was cheaper and less advanced than a radical proposal by Autonetics, but it is nevertheless a fine set for the 1980s and seems quite advanced enough for the 'erks' who will have to look after it. How many of them are familiar with surface-wave devices for pulse-compression signal generation, and pulse-compression matched filters? How many radars previously in use feature amplifiers and oscillators that are microwave integrated circuits? Gunn oscillators are used for both the master oscillator in the exciter and the local oscillator in the TFR receiver. The transmitters for both radars naturally incorporate random frequency-agility, which means they continuously hop from one frequency to another so that hostile receivers are defeated in their efforts to lock-on. Like only the very newest airborne radars both IDS sets have planar phased-array aerials (antennas) with selectable polarisation and beam shape. In other words instead of issuing from a single waveguide at the focus of a parabolic dish, the signals are sent out in sequence from all over a flat aerial, and the actual form and shape of the beam can be altered at will.

Both radars can operate in any of a number of modes. *Off* is self-explanatory. *Ground standby* allows continuous operation at low power to save current and permit adequate cooling with ground fans; it is normally enforced by a switch on one of the main landing gears. *Standby* provides full power to everything except the transmitter high-voltage circuits, and can normally be obtained only in the air. *Test* is a special mode with a dummy load, the BITE (built-in test equipment) automatically detecting 94% of all possible faults and isolating 88.6% to a single LRU (line replaceable unit). An LRU is a single box which can be pulled and replaced in a few seconds by a ground-crewman wearing fur mitts. Older readers may have memories of spending all day, or all night, trying to trace a radar fault so that it could be rectified (for example, with a soldering iron). Tornado does it all for you, in seconds.

The most common airborne mode is *ground mapping,* and this in turn is available in any of four sub-modes, each usable from ground level to the stratosphere. *Ground-map spoiled* is the normal mode, giving a general picture of terrain ahead, with the operator (in most cases the navigator) able to control scan angle and rate. Though certain radar information can be fed to the pilot's HUD (or, even more rarely, moving-map display) the normal presentation is the navigator's Combined Display on which the crystal-clear radar picture is superimposed on a moving-map display. Normally the two coincide. Where necessary the radar picture can update the display, and specific and accurate radar 'fixes' (bearing and distance taken

instantaneously to identified surface features) can automatically refine the aircraft navigation system. In the *ground-map pencil* mode the radar sends out a narrow 'pencil' beam for varous mapping or tracking purposes. *Ground-map wide* gives a one-bar azimuth pattern (in other words a continuous side-to-side scan on a horizontal line fixed in relation to the Earth-surface) with the navigator free to select antenna tilt angle and scan rate. *Ground-map narrow* scans a narrow one-bar azimuth sector usually related to a drift-stabilised centre (in other words to the future track over the ground, which in a strong cross-wind will not be the way the aircraft is pointing).

On-boresight contour mapping eliminates all objects below the stabilised horizontal plane through the aircraft, and supplies video signals from everything that penetrates above this plane, such as a mountain peak, radio mast or tall tree. The scan is a one-bar pattern, stabilised in roll, pitch and yaw to give a clear picture unaffected by manoeuvres. Superimposed on the projected map display this serves as a navaid, and could facilitate picking out the best 'under the radar' route in an unplanned excursion through previously unstudied

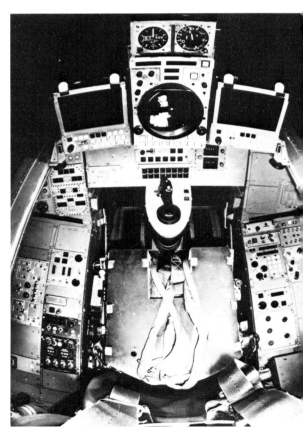

Right: Rear cockpit of aircraft 12, with a number of areas blanked off but showing the central combined display, with manual stick controller, the two flanking tabs (which are graphics computer terminals), the altimeter and Machmeter above the combined display and the side consoles for stores management (left) and nav/com (right)./*BAe*

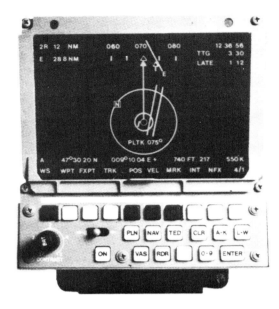

Above: More detail on the navigator's three main displays showing (left) the combined display, with alphanumerics all reading zero, (above left) the tab in the planning format showing the whole mission being built up, and (above right) the in-flight navigation format./*Panavia*

territory. *Height find* is a versatile mode in which tilt angle to an identified surface target is measured, giving a new input to the computer for height computations. A range line appears on the display which the navigator can align over the target.

In the *air-to-ground ranging mode* the antenna is pointed by azimuth/elevation (az/el) commands from the computer, thereafter performing acquisition, range lock-on and tracking automatically against either ground clutter or discrete targets. The output is digital data giving slant range, range-rate (rate of change of range, vital for weapon aiming), az/el pointing angles and a signal to the operator that range tracking has been accomplished. *Lock-on* is a mode in which the computer commands the antenna to point in the right direction, and feeds the radar with the predicted range data, the radar subsequently locking on to the surface target to feed the computer with all range and angle tracking data for weapon aiming. In this mode the antenna does not respond to az/el commands from the computer, but to guard against possible lock-on to the wrong target it does accept a 'lock-on reject' signal that makes it break lock and re-enter the acquisition phase.

Panavia Tornado IDS, Cutaway Drawing Key

1 Pitot head
2 Radome (AEG-Telefunken)
3 Ground mapping/attack radar scanner (Texas Instruments)
4 Terrain following radar scanner (Texas Instruments)
5 Yaw vane
6 Radar processing unit
7 IFF aerial

8 Windscreen rain-repelling air duct
9 Avionics bay
10 Angle of attack probe
11 Canopy release handle
12 Port cannon port
13 Laser ranger and marked target seeker on starboard side (Ferranti)
14 Windscreen (Lucas-Rotax)
15 Instrument panel shroud
16 Cockpit bulkhead
17 Rudder pedals
18 Avionics bay
19 Cannon barrel
20 Nosewheel door
21 Flight refuelling probe (bolt-on)
22 Pilot's head-up display (Smiths)
23 Instrument panel
24 Control column
25 Engine throttles
26 Wing sweep control
27 Command and Stability Augmentation System (CSAS) controller (Marconi-Elliot)
28 Autopilot control panel (Elliot)
29 Pilot's ejection seat (Martin Baker Mk 10)
30 Port 27-mm cannon (Mauser)
31 One piece canopy, open (Kopperschmidt)
32 Rear-view mirrors
33 Canopy jettison charge
34 Navigator's instrument console
35 Port two-dimensional air intake
36 Ammunition feed to starboard cannon
37 Ammunition tank
38 Oxygen bottle
39 Nose undercarriage leg (Dowty Rotol)
40 Twin nosewheels (Dunlop)
41 Cold air inlet
42 Navigator's rear-view mirrors
43 Navigator's instrument display
44 Starboard air intake
45 Navigator's ejection seat (Martin Baker Mk 10)
46 Canopy jack
47 Air-intake ramp jacks (Liebherr Aerotechnik)
48 Formation light

49 Intake variable-area ramp doors
50 Bleed air louvres
51 Supplementary intake doors
52 Air conditioning plant (Normalair-Garrett)
53 Intake control system (Nord-Micro)
54 Intake trunking
55 Wing-root glove fairing
56 Kruger flap, extended
57 Wing pivot sealing fairing
58 Front fuselage bag fuel tank (Uniroyal)
59 Wing sweep actuator (Microtecnica)
60 Wing sweep hydraulic motor
61 Slat and flap combined motor (Microtecnica)
62 Communications aerials
63 Anti-collision light
64 Starboard wing sweep actuator
65 Wing pivot titanium box carry through structure
66 Starboard wing pivot
67 Upper surface wing seal
68 Inboard pylon pivot point
69 Wing torque box
70 Integral fuel tank
71 Full-span leading-edge slats
72 Outboard pylon pivot point
73 Outboard pylon

74 Starboard navigation light
75 Wing tip antenna
76 Spoilers
77 Spoiler jacks
78 Full-span double-slotted flaps
79 Starboard external fuel tank
80 Wing root pneumatic seal
81 Pressurising air inlet
82 HF notch aerial
83 Tailplane mechanical emergency linkage
84 Air-conditioning supply

85 Primary heat exchanger
86 Air outlet
87 Two spar fin construction
88 Fin fuel tank
89 Communications antenna, VOR
90 Electronic tuning controls
91 Passive ECM housing
92 Fin tip antenna, Tacan and V/UHF aerials
93 Tail warning radar (Elettrotecnica)
94 Tail navigation light
95 Rudder

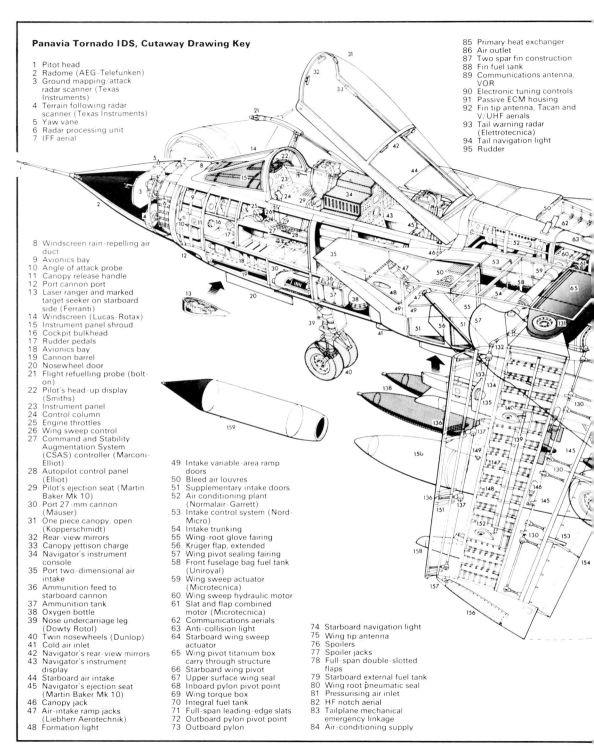

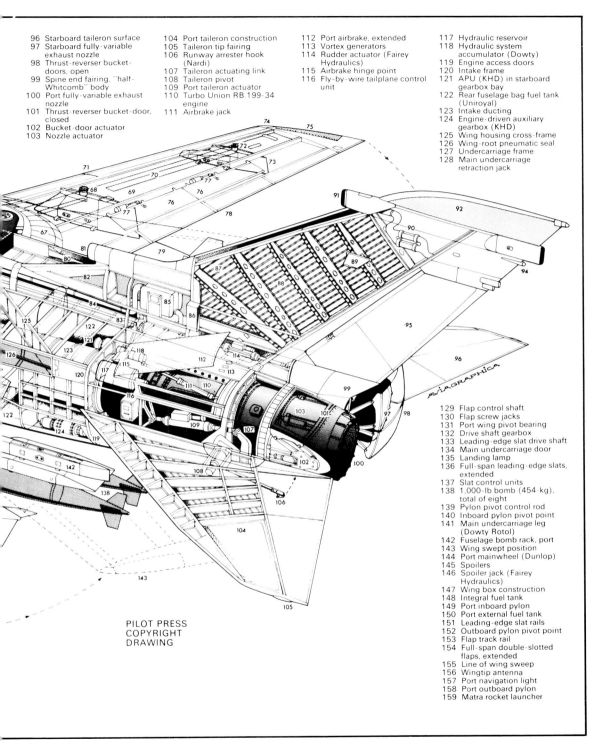

96 Starboard taileron surface
97 Starboard fully-variable exhaust nozzle
98 Thrust-reverser bucket-doors, open
99 Spine end fairing, "half-Whitcomb" body
100 Port fully-variable exhaust nozzle
101 Thrust-reverser bucket-door, closed
102 Bucket-door actuator
103 Nozzle actuator

104 Port taileron construction
105 Taileron tip fairing
106 Runway arrester hook (Nardi)
107 Taileron actuating link
108 Taileron pivot
109 Port taileron actuator
110 Turbo Union RB 199-34 engine
111 Airbrake jack

112 Port airbrake, extended
113 Vortex generators
114 Rudder actuator (Fairey Hydraulics)
115 Airbrake hinge point
116 Fly-by-wire tailplane control unit

117 Hydraulic reservoir
118 Hydraulic system accumulator (Dowty)
119 Engine access doors
120 Intake frame
121 APU (KHD) in starboard gearbox bay
122 Rear fuselage bag fuel tank (Uniroyal)
123 Intake ducting
124 Engine-driven auxiliary gearbox (KHD)
125 Wing housing cross-frame
126 Wing-root pneumatic seal
127 Undercarriage frame
128 Main undercarriage retraction jack

129 Flap control shaft
130 Flap screw jacks
131 Port wing pivot bearing
132 Drive shaft gearbox
133 Leading-edge slat drive shaft
134 Main undercarriage door
135 Landing lamp
136 Full-span leading-edge slats, extended
137 Slat control units
138 1,000-lb bomb (454-kg), total of eight
139 Pylon pivot control rod
140 Inboard pylon pivot point
141 Main undercarriage leg (Dowty Rotol)
142 Fuselage bomb rack, port
143 Wing swept position
144 Port mainwheel (Dunlop)
145 Spoilers
146 Spoiler jack (Fairey Hydraulics)
147 Wing box construction
148 Integral fuel tank
149 Port inboard pylon
150 Port external fuel tank
151 Leading-edge slat rails
152 Outboard pylon pivot point
153 Flap track rail
154 Full-span double-slotted flaps, extended
155 Line of wing sweep
156 Wingtip antenna
157 Port navigation light
158 Port outboard pylon
159 Matra rocket launcher

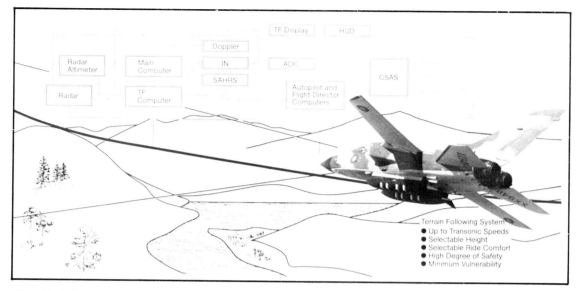

Inside the diagram:

TF Display | HUD

Doppler

Radar Altimeter | Main Computer | IN | ADC

SAHRS | | CSAS

Radar | TF Computer | Autopilot and Flight Director Computers

Terrain Following System
● Up to Transonic Speeds
● Selectable Height
● Selectable Ride Comfort
● High Degree of Safety
● Minimum Vulnerability

Above: Simple diagram showing the TFR 'ski toe' sliding across the terrain ahead, plus a system block diagram./*Panavia*

The *air-to-air tracking* mode is rather similar. When hostile aircraft, or a friendly refuelling tanker, are in the vicinity the computer provides pointing commands and the radar looks in the direction indicated and initiates a range search. After range lock-on the mode switches to angle tracking, sending the data to accept a 'lock-on reject' signal, causing it to break lock and re-enter the acquisiton phase. Otherwise, nothing will deflect it; if lock-on is interrupted due to signal fading or hostile ECM the radar keeps outputting tracking data from the last-known parameters until tracking is resumed.

In April 1978 Panavia announced Radpac (radar package), a Panavia-funded development sponsored by the three governments through allowing the use of modules from the original programme. Dr Fichtmuller, managing director, said: 'Radpac is designed to give the radar a very much augmented air-to-air capability. When associated with the carriage of suitable air-to-air missiles, this gives Tornado IDS a much improved mission capability in the air-to-air roles without compromising air-to-ground capability. It is beamed very much towards the export market, especially towards air forces which require a single avionics solution for the air-to-air and air-to-ground mission'. Radpac would appear a good buy for the four initial customers also, but this had not been announced in mid-1979.

The final mode for the main radar is *beacon,* in which it interrogates friendly aircraft, ground or surface-ship beacons, and displays the replies as alphanumeric codes in the correct positions on the combined display. This gives the identity of each beacon and its bearing and distance from the aircraft. Ground-mapping video is displayed simultaneously. This either provides ground 'fixes' or aim points, or assists rendezvous with friendly aircraft or ships.

The TFR is under the main radar and its phased-array antenna has the vital duty of ensuring that, no matter how close to the ground the Tornado flies, it never hits anything. The polarisation of the signals is circular, to minimise weather problems (because at these shorter wavelengths there is some response from heavy rain and snow). The two-lobe monopulse beam makes a two-bar scan between 8° left and 8° right of the forward centreline and between the elevations of −20° and plus10°. In a banked turn this scan is at first opened up linearly; for faster turn rates it is switched to a figure-of-eight scan with total azimuth of some 15°, the scan being steered into the turn by up to 7° so that the aircraft can see where it is going (which is no longer dead ahead). Full power for TFR is obtained only in the air; on the ground the set is held to the ground-standby mode by a switch on the nose leg (though this can be manually overridden to give the standby mode with the radar under full power but inhibited from firing until Test or TFR are selected.

The ATF (automatic terrain following) subsystem is actually too complex to describe in full. It is a great advance on any F-111 sub-type, and in many ways superior to that developed for the B-1. The TFR and main radar share their own computer – quite separate from the main computer – which handles such tasks as management of the gimbals (antenna bearings) and scan limits, scan mode, displays and, in the case of the

TFR, the complex calculations necessary to maintain safe clearance. The TFR works up to Mach numbers well in excess of unity, over a range of heights and ride comforts selected by the navigator. Ride comfort, a variable pioneered by the F-111, controls the actual profile flown by the aircraft. In a demonstration to a VIP the ride would probably be gentle; going over a sharp ridge, for example, the aircraft would gently dive down the far side, without imposing any vertical acceleration beyond zero-g, like driving fast over a hump-backed bridge. In wartime in dangerous territory the harshest ride would be selected, giving a truly ground-hugging trajectory even across undulating terrain in order to keep as low as possible at all time, the limiting factor being what the crew can take rather than the structural strength and safe life of the aircraft. Like other TFRs, that in the Tornado maintains an imaginary 'ski-toe' shape below and ahead of the aircraft, and makes this ride along and over the obstacles. The shape and position of the ski-toe are controlled by the chosen clearance height, ground speed and ride comfort. Sudden intrusion of anything into the ski-toe causes immediate automatic manoeuvre by the aircraft, and the TFR computer works out whether it is best to pull up or go round an isolated obstruction. How far the TFR can instantly calculate whether it is possible to go between obstructions such as tall masts or balloon cables is probably a classified area.

So much for forward-looking radar. There is also a radar altimeter built into the belly to provide an accurate digital height readout at low levels. This is not fed direct to the backseater, but it is so important to the pilot it can appear on two of his displays, and sometimes on three. Another secondary radar is the doppler, which continuously measures ground speed along four slanting beams reflected from the land or water. This provides digital along-track and across-track velocity data for the main computer. The doppler is one of the two prime navigation systems, the other being the INS (inertial navigation system) which has its own computer to convert accelerations into velocities and thence into distances. A reversionary navigation capability is provided by the SAHR (secondary attitude and heading reference) with a twin-gyro platform and a magnetic detector (a combined magnetic compass and gyro compass), which monitors the attitude and heading but is not normally called upon if other systems work correctly.

There are many other sensors. The most basic is the pitot-static system that measures dynamic pressure at a forward-facing inlet to provide a basis for calculated true airspeed. In the Tornado such calculation is one of the duties of the ADC (air-data computer), which has its own stored programmes to feed the avionics with accurate digital data on the atmospheric environ-ment. Another is the laser rangefinder, which can measure accurate range to a target at the low grazing angles associated with 'under the radar' attacks which would defeat rangefinding by most radars. The laser can also determine the range to a fixpoint more accurately than the radar, because of the very much shorter wavelength used; it can also operate in a passive search mode and locate targets designated by a separate laser fired from another aircraft or by friendly troops on the ground. Not strictly part of Tornado, but highly relevant to it, are such external avionic inputs as those from Tacan, a ground radio navaid; UHF/ADF, another; various other navaids; and the approach aids that enable landings to be made at near-zero weather minima.

Altogether the navaids installed as standard kit in every Tornado form a fairly close approximation — though with less duplicative redundancy — to those in the latest and largest civil airliners. At the risk of causing a riot one could suggest that in modern airliners the P1 or captain sits in haughty management while his peons do the work, and the cynic could suggest it is not very different in Tornado either. Though both cockpits have extremely comprehensive displays, the way the crew actually work in a routine mission is for the pilot to sit in front and watch the scenery, from time to time checking that everything seems to be working properly, while the backseater actually does most of the interfacing between the Tornado and the humans it carries. At the same time a Tornado crew work as a team, and share the overall load pretty evenly.

Before take-off the backseater, who is normally called the navigator in IDS Tornados, supplies the main computer with the complete flight plan, including the take-off location (which is normally already stored from the last flight), all waypoints (the planned turning points), target locations, areas to be avoided, Tacan beacons, known hostile radar or SAM sites, other points of special interest, and map slide references. He also adds spare reference points so that the route can be replanned in flight. He sits in his rear cockpit and taps out the input data via one of his tab-displays, watching the mission grow before his eyes in the form of a luminous yellow-green map display generated electronically on the screen. In this Planning Mode the screen is first made to fit the mission territory, inserting latitude and longitude lines. Waypoints then appear as A, B, C etc, and the target(s) as a small triangle marked with an X. After take-off the system continuously receives information from the sensors, which the navigator studies and occasionally uses to update the system.

As the Tornado streaks down the first leg (the track to the first waypoint) its position is displayed by a small circle moving along the fixed track line. Where

the mission is over land the navigator will have inserted the position of all the identifiable landmarks, or fixpoints, which appear as 1, 2, 3 etc. As the small aircraft-circle approaches each fix, the navigator keeps a sharp lookout for it, and usually tells the pilot who has a better view ahead. The exact position of each fixpoint helps refine the accuracy of the navigation, so that each fix or waypoint should be hit more precisely on the nose. Normally the primary mode of navigation is for the computer to steer the aircraft according to the stored flight plan and the combined inputs from the INS and doppler. The two inputs are combined in a method known as a Kalman-filter software routine to give the most accurate dead-reckoning position, normally suffering from errors less than half those of the INS alone. Even the latter are pretty good by most standards, for an error of half a mile per hour is not exceptional (and Tornado seldom takes anything remotely like an hour to run from one waypoint or fix to the next). In fact, with doppler combined by the Kalman method I doubt that any Tornado on a conventional mission, over land or sea giving good doppler returns, need ever be more than 200 metres off-track even in severe weather, and as the mission progresses this cross-track or along-track error should drop close to zero. A lovely thought that old-time navigators will appreciate.

Normally the mission is flown with one TV-tab in the navigation format and the other spelling out various kinds of helpful information. The nav format is not at all the same as the planning one, though the latter can be restored at the touch of a key. The nav-format is based on aircraft present position, shown as a small fixed circle at the centre, around which is a 'circle of 95 per cent certainty', and a much larger range circle with a boxed N on it to show the direction of true north. Superimposed on this is a vertical line passing through the 12 o'clock position to show the current track, read off a scale at the top of the screen. Thus, changing heading causes the scale to slide past the track line, while the boxed N moves smoothly around the range circle. PLTK (planned track) is spelt out digitally, with parallel lines scaled a fixed distance apart to show cross-track error (if any), as well as the next waypoint, the next track beyond the waypoint and many other things as well. Blocks of data in the upper corners show (left) distance in NM (nautical miles) to the next fixpoint and to the next waypoint, and (right) the system time (which may or may not also be the precise time of day), the time to the next waypoint and the time the aircraft is early or late.

Even this merely scratches the surface of the navigation process. Between the tab-displays is the big Combined Display on which present position is seen at

Above: Comparative take-off pictures of 12 (left, with eight 1,000lb bombs) and two-pilot No 11 (right). The large wing pylons swivel to remain aligned with the airflow. Nose leg is extendable for short-field take-offs./*Panavia*

the centre of a detailed coloured topographical map and/or a detailed radar display. The moving radar video picture ought to lie precisely upon the moving map, and any discrepancy helps the navigator study the situation as shown by the INS and doppler; with at least four inputs, quite apart from seeing fixpoints with his own eyes, it ought to take a prolonged effort to become even the slightest bit lost. At any time it is possible to provide yet further backups by inputting Tacan figures, radar beacon positions, UHF/ADF bearings and even fixes from the nose laser. And all this is quite apart from continuous steering information presented to the pilot, most immediately via his HUD. Old-time aircrew (like the author) who learned their trade with pencils and plotting charts, and bundles of tatty maps in cramped cockpits – and to whom a computer was a small box with a roller blind and hand-knobs for solving triangle-of-velocities pro-

blems – find this age of electronic luminescent displays exciting indeed. It does not mean one iota less skill or attention from today's aircrew.

Of course, the enemy will do their best to interfere with this serene progress, though precisely how the Tornado handles the various threats is classified. According to *The International Countermeasures Handbook* the standard fit on IDS Tornado includes a Marconi AD.980 ECM central suppression unit, an Italian Elettronica EL-73 radar warning receiver and the 'Marconi/Decca/Plessey Ajax X-band 6-12 GHz jamming pod developed by the Royal Aircraft Establishment'. This may or may not be true, but it would be odd if there was no provision for internal built-in receiving and jamming in so new an aircraft designed for use in sophisticated electronic environments. The aerials near the top of the fin look similar to those of the GEC-Marconi ARI.18228 analog-controlled RWR (radar warning receiver) carried by other RAF tactical aircraft. All that can be said officially is 'The aircraft carries a comprehensive suite of ECM equipment that will warn the crew of any impending threat'. There is an ad hoc warning display in both cockpits.

Probably the only other major area that must be included in this chapter is weapon delivery. It has already been mentioned that targets are marked on the tabs as small triangles lettered X. These come up fast, because attacks might be expected to be attacked at full throttle, and at low levels Tornado is probably the fastest aircraft in the world. But for precise delivery either the weapon must be guided or it must free-fall from an exact position relative to the target. One way to do it is for the target to be acquired visually by the pilot in his HUD, whereupon he can aim and release bombs by conventional methods. Another way is to make a blind attack on the radar. A third is to use the laser to search for a target marked by troops or friendly aircraft or other platforms. In each case laser/radar or laser/HUD is likely to be used for exact ranging. And 'conventional methods' today seldom mean that the pilot aims the aircraft and releases bombs manually. The normal mode is for release to be by the computer, according to the navigation sensors and laser/radar ranging, because the computer is much more accurate and automatically takes account of the aircraft flight vector, wind velocity, drift angle, aircraft attitude and precise trajectory equations of each type of store.

When guided missiles are used these can fly to the target by several methods. Anti-radar Martel (AS.37) flies by itself towards hostile radar emissions of the correct wavelength if the latter are so amateur as to permit it. TV-guided Martel (AJ.168) is steered by the backseater, and in Tornado this can be done beautifully using an appropriate format on one of the tabs. Kormoran, the first large guided missile to be fired from Tornado, is an anti-ship missile with self-homing capability, so it is a 'launch and leave' weapon needing no interface with the crew. There are other guided weapons that could well be fired by Tornado, such as the Paveway 'smart bombs' which home on laser radiation from the target. These are normally matched to a laser wavelength of 1.064 microns, and it would be reasonable to assume that Tornado's inbuilt laser is of this wavelength (which is known to be one of the wavelengths of Nd/YAG lasers), obviating the need to carry a Pave Penny or similar designator as an external store.

Perhaps I should add a little on the IDS aircraft in two other roles, air-to-air and reconnaissance. In the former it is clearly an outstanding aircraft compared with any other known blind first-pass attack platform, especially with Radpac fitted. Basic air-to-air weapons include pairs of Sidewinders on the sides of the inboard wing pylons and the two guns. Subject to the confines of geometry and aerodynamics (for example, keeping a close eye on wing deflections) there is no reason why augmented loads of air-to-air weapons should not be carried, not excluding the large Sparrow and its derivatives, though drag would be greater than that of the recessed installations of the ADV described later. This is a role in which increased-thrust versions of the RB.199 engine, so far of little interest to the Tornado customers, could be used with advantage.

As for reconnaissance, Tornado could obviously do a superb job in this role, either as a specialist aircraft or – as the existing customers plan to do – used with external multi-sensor pods. One of the chief customers, the Luftwaffe, needed modern reconnaissance aircraft quickly and bought the special-purpose RF-4E Phantom; the RAF uses pods on Phantoms, Jaguars and Harriers, while the AMI uses the rather limited RF-104G and G91R. Tornado offers dramatically greater radius and carrying power than any of these aircraft, and it would appear logical for as many as possible of the customers to get together on a really effective modern multi-sensor pod tailored to the Tornado. Unlike the F-111, which has great difficulty in carrying external pods of large size and which has been subjected to two extremely costly rebuild programmes to carry sensors internally, the Tornado IDS could carry the most comprehensive reconnaissance pod whilst retaining full attack capability.

Even this by no means exhausts the long list of human/machine interfaces that enable the IDS Tornado to fly its missions. For example, the tabs can do much more than I have so far described. In the reconnaissance role they can present the backseater with readouts from the various sensors, and these can take the form of video pictures, if necessary with particular items ringed or annotated, and various kinds of alphanumeric or other information. The tabs can also present a diverse array of fault indications, usually as instantly prepared alphanumeric readouts going into considerable detail. It would be logical to assume that, in so modern an aircraft, the backseater can interface with such displays either by his multifuncion keyboards or by touchwires or other direct inputs on the display face itself. (It has been disclosed that Warton is at present testing the Marconi Digilux "fly by touch" system in which the display is crisscrossed by fine IR beams which are broken when the backseater touches the display at the appropriate spot with something more pointed than a gloved forefinger.)

Technology certainly exists to offer successively refined information. Thus – and in the absence of unclassified information this is speculation – the first warning of a fault would be a brilliant illuminated caption panel giving broadbrush information. The next stage would be to call up more detailed information on one of the tabs, and this might mean temporarily erasing the navigation display though there would probably be one display in the alphanumeric mode during most of the mission. With really large computer capacity it should be possible to present quite detailed information on most faults, and possible remedial action by the crew. There might even be a situation in which the readout says *EJECT*!

Tornado
in Service

So far this book has tended to revolve around technical matters, as must any book on such a subject. Even Tornado Pilot's Notes, when they are finally issued to the troops, will be unintelligible in places to chaps who retired or were promoted to 'fly a desk' as recently as five years ago. In the final chapter I will return for a second look at the total revolution in technology brought by the electronic age. Thousands of people, an increasing proportion of them in uniform, have for several years been progressing into this new era as part of the Tornado programme. At the same time it is only common sense that this vitally important aircraft has been designed to fit, so far as this is possible, into the existing air forces. Somebody said of a different aircraft 'You don't have to be a PhD in physics to fly it; but it helps'. This underlines the fact that the customers have been facing problems more fundamental than they have been used to.

Unlike every previous aircraft Tornado has from the outset been tailored not only to meet the quantified requirements of four customers in three countries but to give a flexibility beyond them. These customers have not forgotten about it during the past ten years of development. They have been most intimately involved at every stage, at first chiefly sitting round tables and since 1975 in getting to grips with the product. Altogether the three-nation, four-customer planning has been on an unprecedented scale, and it has gone almost without a hitch, which doubtless explains why it has been ignored by the media.

It is worth emphasising the intimacy of effort between the prime contractor Panavia, the three governments (represented via NAMMA) and the four initial air forces. I must particularly mention the gigantic input from CSDU, the RAF Central Servicing and Development Unit. This did not happen in the past. Even after World War II, there was often antipathy between contractors and customers, and it was by no means unusual for a prototype to be rejected by the government test pilots. Indeed, I recall a dinner at the Aeroplane & Armament Experimental Establishment, Boscombe Down, at which a silver-haired officer said 'It is our job to pick faults'. Older readers will recall many instances where the customer threw something out because of its poor performance, unacceptable handling or even the bad layout of the cockpit. No problem; there were always plenty of fall-back programmes. How different today! There is no fall-back programme to Tornado, nor should one be needed (though competition is highly desirable, as the Soviet Union continually demonstrates in its aircraft programmes). For anyone to 'reject' Tornado would have been unthinkable. It seems to me obviously a better method for contractor and customer to collaborate as closely as possible to make sure the final product meets all requirements. Yet aviation is still an art, and one has only to recall the closest parallel to Tornado that exists in the Western world, the F-111, to see that success can be hard to achieve. With Tornado, Europe has been blessed with tremendous good fortune that could never have been guaranteed in advance – though a will to make it happen does help.

Early prototype flying was naturally a close-knit family affair by aircraft continually subject to small changes and packed with instrumentation. It had to be so, in order to get the necessary answers with minimal time and risk. Despite their cost, the earlier Tornado prototypes are so unlike the production aircraft that they will not be issued to the squadrons. This is inevitable; it is beyond human capability to make the first few prototypes closely resemble the production machine. The first F-15 Eagles, for example, are so unlike the production aircraft that they could not even be used as ground trainers, and they now serve as static exhibits or as additions to 'The Boneyard' at Davis-Monthan. Some early Tornados may end up the same way, though work has been found for all of them so far. Only the last four of the six pre-series aircraft are being refurbished for delivery as regular aircraft for the inventory, cutting the number of true production IDS aircraft for the initial customers from 644 to 640. At the time of writing, three batches of production aircraft had been ordered: July 1976, 40; May 1977, 110; June 1979, 164, a total of 314.

Apart from extensive planning, the first direct customer involvement with the hardware began on 26 November 1975, when Fritz Soos took off in aircraft 01 for a 50-minute work-out. Soos was not then a Panavia pilot but a civilian test pilot employed by the German government, who had previously completed the MRCA aircrew training course. He knew what to expect, of course, yet it was still his task to represent the customer and see if he could find anything to criticise. When he came down the steps afterwards he wore the largest possible grin, and this was not merely because 'Fred' Rammensee, MBB Chief Test Pilot, gave him a bouquet. Next in line were Klaus Koglin,

Above: First Tornado in service hands was No 12, delivered to Boscombe Down on 3 February 1978. With wings at 26° it can, the pilots assure me, 'be overloaded and still fly like a Canberra'./*BAe*

Above right: Tornado 11 carrying the MW-1 dispenser, a weapon that other tactical aircraft cannot carry. Each of its four sections has 28 double-ended tubes, fired in rapid sequence at very low level to project armour-killing bomblets horizontally to each side. A proportion may have delay fuses and behave as mines./*MBB*

Britain's Sqn Ldr Ron Burrows and Wg Cdr Clive Rustin, and Italy's Lt-Cols Cesare Calzone and Pasquale Garriba.

In the subsequent three years numerous flights were made by these and other government test pilots, while numerous senior officers – including the chiefs of staff of all the customer air forces – and government ministers also flew, or flew in, a number of prototypes. Eventually Panavia produced a book called 'Tornado Quotes', and this has become fatter and more impressive with each edition. The quotations do not come from Panavia people or advertising copywriters, though they read as if they might. They were said by skilled professionals whose opinions cannot be bought, and it is fair to reproduce one or two here:

'For me this was a perfect first flight ... ' Lt-Cdr Dietrich Seeck, Marineflieger test pilot.

'Compared with other aircraft the Tornado's handling qualities represent ... a previously unheard-of optimum' Lt-Col Karl-Heinze Steuer, Luftwaffe test pilot.

'I found the aircraft very manoeuvrable, and it behaved perfectly with one engine cut to idling' Gen Dino Ciarlo, Aeronautica Militare Italiano Chief of Staff.

'The aircraft has exceeded all my expectations. Response to pilot inputs is very fast and very accurate at all speeds and at all sweep angles. I wouldn't have expected this kind of agility, particularly in the low-level high-speed regime' Gen Gerhard Limberg, Luftwaffe Chief of Staff.

'The ride was extremely good, smooth and as steady as a rock – very impressive. It enables the crew to concentrate on the job in hand rather than on flying ... ' Air Chief Marshal Sir Douglas Lowe, UK Controller of Aircraft.

'As docile as a St Bernard but as fast, aggressive and powerful as a panther when challenged ... a successful one-man operation would be impossible ... the F-104 chase aircraft reported heavy turbulence which we didn't notice at all ... one can't but be enthusiastic; to my knowledge there is nothing comparable' Admiral Rudolf Deckert, Commander Marinefliegerdivision.

'The Tornado has better handling than any aircraft I have ever flown' Air Chief Marshal Sir Michael Beetham, RAF Chief of the Air Staff.

'I am enthusiastic, and I only wish I could fly this aircraft long enough to try out all its capabilities ... ' Gen Fulvio Ristori, AMI Deputy Chief of Staff.

Of course, perhaps none of these people know what they are talking about; maybe the experts of television and the newspapers are more accurate in their opinions, but I doubt it. Had more of the latter bothered to visit the crews of the Tornado Evaluation Squadron at Boscombe Down, for example, they might have found the tremendous enthusiasm of the

people who actually live with Tornado infectious. Most of the time these true experts are busy studying specific things, but when asked they can make considered broad assessments, two of the fundamental ones being – and I quote from Clive Rustin and his colleagues Sqn Ldr Roger Beazley and Flt Lt Don Thomas – that crew comfort in the crucial tree-top transonic regime is of a quality 'not previously experienced in this environment', and the backseaters consider their equipment provides 'a capability far in advance of anything within our previous experience'.

It is a pity that reasons of security preclude going into detail on how the Tornado shapes up to other aspects of its many tasks, such as its mission radii with particular weapon loads, or its electronic performance. It has been stated the IDS aircraft can fly combat missions out of 'any 3,000ft strip'. With typical weapon load the hi-lo-lo-hi interdiction mission radius is given as 750 nautical miles (864 miles, 1390km) with the 'lo' part flown at full throttle at 200ft (60m). The ferry mission is given as 2,100 nautical miles (2,418 miles, 3,892km). The LLDF (low-level discomfort factor), measured as the number of 0.5g bumps per minute at high-subsonic speed at sea level is given as about 0.8, compared with 5.4 for the F-104, 12.2 for the F-15, 12.9 for the F-16 (the F-18 would be at least as high as this) and 15.0 for the F-4. Any interdiction pilot will appreciate the significance of these figures. The last three are well up within the 'very uncomfortable' region where crew performance is severely degraded, though all are in service, or planned, for the interdiction mission in Europe.

From 1976 Tornados increasingly operated away from the Panavia test bases, and were positioned at various air force and Marineflieger bases for anything from a day to several months. Prolonged evaluations were made of operational readiness, turnround time, reliability and maintainability. Exercises were mounted to prove operations in and out of hardened shelters, initially at RAF Bentwaters (a USAF base) and Schleswig (Marineflieger). No problems were encountered. Increasingly Tornados participated in public air displays, with minimal ground support, and have never yet missed their slot in the programme.

In April 1978 Panavia set up a Product Support Directorate, charged with the mammoth task of providing and managing the Tornado spares, ground equipment, technical documentation (hundreds of tons of it) and industrial overhaul facilities for the four customers. One obvious result is logistics commonality, so often conspicuously lacking in NATO; it is even better than in the F-104 programme, and in terms of size is several times larger than the European F-16 programme. The latter is based upon American equipment, but the Tornado AGE (aerospace ground equipment) is European. Even procuring the AGE was a gigantic business. The method was called MAGERD (MRCA AGE Requirement Data) and every item had to pass through seven parts called Part A to Part G before it could be produced for the customer. This involved hand tools, rigs, hydraulic power trolleys and test gear from hand-gauges to the ATS (automatic test station).

ATS deserves special mention because, while it is easily the biggest programme for automatic test equipment in Europe, it is an exceptional effort by any standard. Each ATS is a computerised installation able to handle complete and rapid testing and fault-diagnosis of all Tornado avionics, a total of more than 100 different types of 'black box'. More than 100 ATS will be installed in the second-line maintenance units of the four user air forces. Tornado has its own built-in test

equipment (BITE) integrated into an On-Board Checkout and Monitoring System (OCAMS) which, as explained previously, tells the air or ground crew instantly of any fault and isolates it to a particular LRU (Line-Replaceable Unit, in other words a box replaced by a tradesman on the flight-line). But nobody is going to junk the LRU removed from the aircraft; it will probably cost dozens of times more than a domestic TV set. Instead it is taken to the nearest ATS and in seconds the fault is analysed to a particular card or printed circuit, so the junked part is the irreducible minimum, of small cost. The ATS comprises four stations, one for LF (low frequency), one for RF (radio frequency), one for microwaves and one for video signal processing. The ATS programme was developed and managed by a three-nation consortium led by Marconi Avionics.

ATS is one of the larger examples of Tornado infrastructure that ought to be applicable to other types of aircraft in the late 1980s and beyond. Though Tornado is the nearest thing yet to a 'one-plane air force' (sorry, Fairchild Republic, it knocks the F-105 into a cocked hat), other types are going to be needed. In the case of the three Panavia nations discussions have been going on for several years about a fighter jokingly called the 'Spitwulf 190' but actually known by a different Requirement designation in each country (in Britain it was Air Staff Target 403).

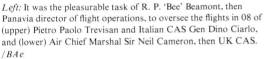

Left: It was the pleasurable task of R. P. 'Bee' Beamont, then Panavia director of flight operations, to oversee the flights in 08 of (upper) Pietro Paolo Trevisan and Italian CAS Gen Dino Ciarlo, and (lower) Air Chief Marshal Sir Neil Cameron, then UK CAS. */BAe*

Above: Two important backseaters were (left) Sir Michael Beetham, newly appointed CAS, aboard dual 03 on 26 September 1977, and (right) Sir Peter Terry, VCAS, aboard 08. Note the full complement of displays facing Sir Peter, who had John Cockburn, senior avionics development pilot, up front./*BAe*

Whatever may finally be adopted, it or they will emerge into a world strongly influenced by Tornado, and this is especially the case with AGE and the ATS in particular.

Many of the readers of this book will later make the acquaintance of Tornado. They will rightly have concluded that it is an order of magnitude later in technology and general sophistication than anything they have previously experienced. But there is no need to be apprehensive; Tornado is an outstanding example of the modern combat aircraft designed to meet numerically specified maintenance times. One recalls some of the (actually far simpler) aircraft of the 1950s with horror, because it was only after they had been built that it was discovered that to get at some

trivial item you had to remove the engine or wing. Tornado is rather better than this, and has to be because skilled man-hours are no longer cheap. Almost 40 per cent of the whole exterior is made up of access panels, and every panel used on normal line servicing can be opened in a second or two without using any tool. As far as possible all the thousands of items inside need no routine inspection or adjustment whatever. I have already explained the degree to which faults are automatically indicated and isolated by BITE and other on-board systems, and the use of LRUs virtually eliminates either repair on base or calibration of the fresh LRU after it has been installed.

As in the airlines, 'on-condition' philosophy has been followed wherever possible, which is almost the same as 'let well alone'. Pre-flight service before the first flight of the day requires no more than a check of the tyres, various fluid contents (such as fuel, oil, hydraulics and lox) and any exterior damage that may have happened overnight. For turnround between flights two panels are opened for refuelling, four for oil checks and another (the central maintenance panel) gives an instant check on LRU status. Lox level is also shown on a cockpit gauge, and hydraulic fluid level and accumulator pressures are displayed on skin-mounted gauges. No tools are required for any operation on the flight line. The on-board APU is used for starting engines and providing ground power. After

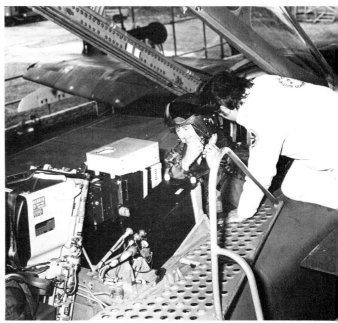

Left: Rammensee is probably holding a rolled-up presentation scroll as he congratulates the Commander, Marineflieger, Admiral Rudolf Deckert, after their work-out in aircraft 11 from the MFG base at Jagel, near Schleswig, on 15 September 1977./*MFG*

Above: Perhaps the ultimate 'customer', who had a 69-minute flight in No 11 at Manching with Friedrich Soos on 14 March 1978, was Gen Heinz Birkenbeil, General Manager of NAMMA. Note the general's maps and kneepad on the right tab display./*Panavia*

Above right: Another view showing Mk 10A seats, navigator displays, ladder platform, canopy and wing position at 16°. Aircraft is No 12, crewed by David Eagles and Admiral Sir Edward Ashmore, Chief of UK Defence Staff, 24 August 1977./*BAe*

the last flight of the day the total of servicing again comprises damage or defect assessment, checking fluid levels and replenishing where necessary. Where the aircraft has to be declared unserviceable and subjected to repair or overhaul, the immediate accessibility of everything will be a source of delight. The main windshield hinges forward for access to instruments. The radome hinges 180° to the right, and so does the complete main radar aerial group. All engine items, bar none, are accessible from doors on the underside, and if the engines have to be pulled they drop down in a remarkably short number of minutes.

The first Tornado to be permanently in customer's hands was P.12, flown by David Eagles from Warton to Boscombe Down on 3 February 1978. The British

government test centre, the A&AEE, is one of the three designated OTCs (Official Test Centres) for the Tornado, the others being Deutsches Bundeswehr E-Stelle (Test Centre) 61 at Manching and the Reparto Sperimentale di Volo at Pratica di Mare, near Rome. Aircraft No 11 was handed over to E-Stelle 61 on 28 March 1979.

As in the rest of the programme the work of the OTCs has been planned as a tri-national integrated effort. The tasks are to complete the customer evaluation of Tornado in its operational roles and to train instructors for subsequent aircrew conversion. It has also provided experience for a nucleus of skilled ground tradesmen who will probably be instructors at the Tornado Ground School before this appears in print. As in the contractors' flight development programme each OTC is assigned specific areas for its particular attention – those for Boscombe are Armament, Handling, and Navigation and Radio, which seems to cover almost the lot – but they do not work in isolation. Air Cdre Brownlow, A&AEE Commandant, explains 'The whole programme is carefully integrated. Our pilots are flying on different tasks at the German and Italian OTCs, just as we have German and Italian pilots here at Boscombe. And we have Service crews from all three countries flying on contractor joint trials at the Panavia airfields in conjunction with the civil test crews'. I believe this is a new development, certainly on an international scale.

While OTC flying was still in full swing in 1978, many other things were happening. Link-Miles and their continental partners were busy with the flight simulators, and nav/attack system simulator, production examples of which will obviously go to all customers. Surprisingly, no CGI (computer-generated image) system was specified for this, to present the harassed occupant with an external view better than those created by running a sensing head across a terrain model. Doubtless a CGI will eventually find its way into the simulators at the Tornado bases. As an interesting incidental, BAe Warton designed their own combat simulator, though this is a different animal from the normal crew-training simulator. The combat simulator is primarily a design tool to establish numerical values for crucial factors in air-to-air and air-to-ground operations, but it is amazingly realistic. Though it uses only one dome, thus saving costs over the two-dome American examples, the BAe manoeuvre attack simulator – as it is called – has such refinements as building in light-dimming as the pilot pulls extreme g to simulate onset of blackout, and convincing buffet as he flies through the wake of a hostile aircraft.

Continuing the totally tri-national approach to the training of squadron crews, a study group by the four customers not only endorsed the general philosophy but laid the foundation for joint effort on a scale never before seen within NATO. Lip-service has always been paid to eliminating the almost universal incom-

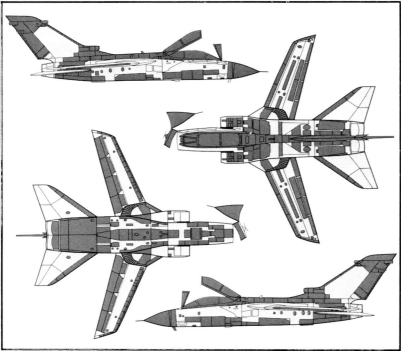

Above: The AOC Strike Command, Sir David Evans, who flew 03 on 16 October 1978, shows the standard UK aircrew clothing with ankle and above-knee garters, PEC (personal equipment connector) resting on left leg, and writing pens in arm pocket./*BAe*

Left: Design for maintenance: four views of the IDS Tornado showing how much of the exterior is covered with access panels./*Panavia*

The extent of American interest in Tornado can be gauged from these photographs:
Right: Lt-Gen Thomas P. Stafford, USAF DCoS for R&D, with John Cockburn, BAe Warton senior avionics development pilot, before the general's 74-minute evaluation of 08 on 13 December 1978;
Far right: the US President, Jimmy Carter, discusses the aircraft with Gen William J. Evans, C-in-C AFCENT (Allied Air Forces, Central Europe) (note MW-1 fitted to 04 in background);

patibilities between NATO forces, but Tornado has for once opened the way to true integration as good as anything seen in the Warsaw Pact. (One wonders how far the process would have gone had it not been clearly shown to offer large financial, as well as military, benefits.) The study group recommended tri-national Tornado training at two levels, beginning with a Joint Operational Conversion Unit (JOCU) at RAF Cottesmore and subsequent weapons training at the AMI (Italian AF) base at Decimomannu in Sardinia. Apart from renaming JOCU the Tri-national Tornado Training Establishment (TTTE, which hardly rolls off the tongue), the first proposal has gone through most successfully, and Cottesmore will be in business when this book appears in 1980.

Previously in Rutland, Cottesmore became part of Leicestershire when England's smallest county lost its identity. More than £12 million has been spent on the base to fit it for its new role (it had previously been planned as the first to have TSR.2, F-111K and AFVG!), including a hardstand for 30 aircraft, an engine test centre, new simulator centres, system training buildings and even extra runway turnoffs to take advantage of Tornado's short landing run. More than 40 Tornados, mainly of the two-pilot type, will be supplied from all three Panavia members and assigned at random to three Flying Training Squadrons, each of which will have a commanding officer of different nationality. Students will again be posted to any squadron, as will the instructors and specialist staff, the only common factor being the standard syllabus which lasts four months and includes 60 hours flying. Pilot and navigator training was planned in the finest detail by the Aircrew Training Course Design Team under W/Cdr Don Oakden. The post of Chief Instructor will rotate between the RAF and Luftwaffe.

On the other hand the plan for a joint weapons conversion unit has been replaced as this is written by separate national schools. Decimomannu was found to lack airfield capacity and weapons range capacity, and will be used only by the AMI. Britain and Germany planned to set up a school at RAF Honington, but though this unit is going ahead the German government announced in May 1979 it would withdraw from this joint effort 'for various reasons, one of them financial'. A Luftwaffe spokesman said the 'situation could change', and there is no news of a German Tornado weapons school.

According to Air Vice-Marshal John Langer, RAF, co-chairman of the Tri-National Steering Committee, 'It would be foolish to pretend that it has been easy to evolve a system that meets the training requirements of the three air forces and the Marineflieger, and some compromise has been inevitable. However, the will to succeed is great because we are all convinced that joint Tornado training is not only a significant milestone in

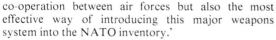

Above: Soos appears to be the pilot briefing the Chief of Staff, US Navy, Admiral Thomas B. Hayward, in December 1978;
Above right: Gen Lou Allen Jr, USAF Chief of Staff, accompanied by VCoS Lt-Gen Howard Fish, closely examined aircraft 12 at RAF Wittering on 6 April 1979; *Right:* on 5 June 1979 Gen Alton D. Slay, Commander, USAF Systems Command, flew 08 at Boscombe Down with Cockburn in the front seat (briefing the general is George McAuley, Warton navigator/*Panavia, MoD, Associated Press.*

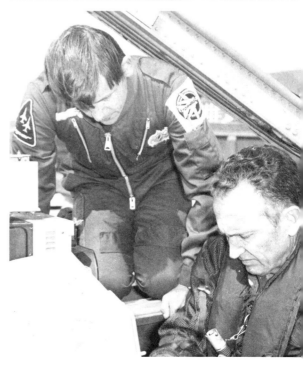

co-operation between air forces but also the most effective way of introducing this major weapons system into the NATO inventory.'

Though the customers appear unworried, there has been severe slippage in the whole programme at the manufacturing level, which in early 1979 was put at 'six to eight months' but actually seems – from study of earlier predictions – to be more than double this period. One should not forget that originally the objective was to bring the aircraft into service in 1975, as reflected in the designation MRA-75; and in July 1970 the British Minister of State for Defence said 'I would expect the MRCA to start coming into service in the second half of the decade'. This makes 'six to eight months' look like an inaccurate assessment. Panavia intend to catch up lost time during production.

Above: Italian 05 on the approach, with tanks and Ajax pods. Landing speed is slower than civil jetliners, and on touchdown the pilot can select anti-skid brakes, reversers, spoilers, airbrakes and hook!/*Aeritalia*

As it is, the first aircraft for the first customer — the Marineflieger — will not be delivered until 'the latter half of 1981', with the first operational unit beginning conversion in January 1982. The Marineflieger is to receive 112 aircraft with very small differences in equipment fit, to replace three fighter-bomber squadrons equipped with 96 F-104Gs and one tac-recon unit with 25 RF-104Gs, organised into two wings: MFG 1 at Schleswig and MFG 2 at Eggbek. The Luftwaffe is to receive 212 aircraft from 1981-2 to replace the present force of 430 F/TF/RTF-104G Starfighters which at present equip four geschwadern (wings): JaboG 31 at Norvenich (2 ATAF), JaboG 32 at Lechfeld (4 ATAF), JaboG 33 at Buchel (2 ATAF) and JaboG 34 at Memmingen (4 ATAF).

Details of recipient RAF units have not been made public, but the Tornado IDS, designated Tornado GR.1 (GR = ground-attack and reconnaissance), will replace the Vulcan and Buccaneer. A total of 220 aircraft will be received, beginning some time after the start of deliveries to MFG 2 in 1982. It is, in passing, worth commenting that all-weather precision delivery was the intended role of TSR.2, due to be received by the RAF (at Cottesmore, as it happens) in 1968, and of the F-111K, due to be received in the same year; and when the British government rejected the proposed Spey-Mirage IVA as a TSR.2 replacement

instead of the F-111K it was officially stated 'this aircraft could not have been delivered until two years after the F-111, and the RAF cannot wait until 1970'. Even a British politician might have some difficulty explaining why it actually has to wait until after 1982. For the record, existing Vulcan squadrons, all in Strike Command's 1 Group, are Nos 9, 35, 44, 50, 101 and 617, typically with 12 aircraft each, while the Buccaneer force comprises Nos 12 and 208 Squadrons at Honington, each with 24 aircraft, and Nos 15 and 16 Squadrons at Laarbruch. It is interesting that the 220 Tornado GR1s will outnumber the existing Vulcan/Buccaneer force, besides being individually vastly more capable.

The Aeronautica Militare Italiano plans to receive 100 IDS Tornados, though no date for the start of deliveries has been made public. Only 54 aircraft are planned to be assigned to combat units, the most efficient arrangement financially being three mixed combat (attack)/reconnaissance squadrons each with

89

18 aircraft. An alternative being studied is three combat squadrons each with 14 aircraft and a specialised reconnaissance squadron with 12. An additional 12 dual-control Tornados will equip an operational training school (which will not necessarily be at Decimomannu). The only existing unit named as a likely recipient is 6 Wing at Ghedi, with F-104Gs. The intention is that the remaining 34 aircraft shall be 'kept in reserve and used during maintenance and attrition'.

There is little point in speculating on export sales of the Tornado, beyond noting that the aircraft was eliminated from the short lists of Australia and Canada. Both countries had, at the time of writing, fallen for the apparently lower price of the proposed F-18 or F-16, the Canadians in particular making it clear that price was the only reason for rejection of the European aircraft. As far as the public record is concerned, not enough has been said for any judgement to be made on the rightness of the decision of these potential customers to eliminate Tornado. In large deals of this kind politics and industrial offsets play a large and often commanding part in the decision-making process. It does seem obvious, however, that

Above: A fine picture of 03 and 08 at high speed with wings at 68°; 03 has tanks, eight low-drag bombs and Ajax pods, while 08 has a number of unusual features under the nose. The tailerons are the only possible place for the underside serial number./*BAe*

Above right: Apart from the gap under the rudder on the two more distant aircraft these three German-assembled Tornados might be on an operational mission./*MBB*

both countries are happy to end up with an aircraft operationally less-capable than Tornado, less well developed and probably more likely to suffer technical problems and cost-escalation. Put another way, it seems short-sighted to discard the fully developed and ideally suited aircraft for a supposed 'cheaper' machine which even on paper cannot fly the same missions and which — all common-sense and past experience indicates — will not prove to be cheaper at all.

One extremely interesting prospect in 1979 was the US Air Force. This has lately received three excellent aircraft, the F-15 air superiority fighter, A-10A close-support platform and F-16 light tactical fighter. What it does not have is anything like Tornado — other than

the ageing and cumbersome F-111 — able to carry formidable loads into heavily defended territory by day or night in all weather and place them with pinpoint accuracy. The A-10A is deficient in performance, navigation and terrain-following, the F-15 is deficient in navigation, terrain-following and crew comfort, and in any case is optimised for the air-to-air mission, and the F-16 is even more limited, though a superficially attractive machine which was never designed for such a role. Since 1976 the gap has been recognised by an evolving requirement for an Enhanced Tactical Fighter (ETF). In December 1978 Lt-Gen Tom Stafford, DCOS for Research and Development (the former Astronaut), visited Britain and flew the Hawk, Harrier and Tornado as part of a serious evaluation to see if aircraft existed that could form the basis for an ETF. His involvement with Tornado was predictably intense and favourable. On 21 March 1979 Panavia announced it had 'chosen Grumman Aerospace Corporation as its partner in submitting the Tornado all-weather combat aircraft to the USAF ...' Though the USAF has budgetary problems like anyone else, my money is on Tornado winning this particular deal, if it actually comes to

pass. When you match it against the requirement it is hard to see any other horse in the race, though the paper ones are marvellous.

A final topic worth discussion is what the RAF will use as its future EW (electronic-warfare) platform. There seems little alternative to the long-established American ALQ-99 system, in the two-man crew version as installed in the USAF's EF-111A. Use of the F-111A is clearly out; in fact I think the USAF is going to be hard-pressed to find enough airframes to carry the ALQ-99 systems and keep the combat-ready wings of the D,E and F versions at full strength. The four-man crew as adopted by the EA-6B Prowler of the US Navy is in my view a non-starter for at least five reasons, as is the use of the Tornado airframe. Surely the obvious platform is the tough Buccaneer, which has already been studied in this role. The RAF has enough low-time Buccaneers to take care of the whole requirement, if Tornados were allowed to replace the younger Buccaneers first. It should not be long before we hear something about funding a trial installation for a new electronic-warfare Buccaneer. Such a platform might even be adopted by the Luftwaffe, Marineflieger and other customers.

The Air Defence Variant

When is an MRCA not an MRCA? This is the rather pointless quibble that some observers of the aviation scene appear to find a total stumbling-block. The argument runs: 'If it is a multi-role aircraft it can do everything, so how can anyone need a special version?' One might as well say that building a particularly good family car eliminates the need for a convertible or an estate. The fact is – and it is not really difficult to understand – that it is possible to adapt almost every modern aircraft so that it can perform especially well in a particular role. Tornado IDS is indeed an outstandingly versatile aircraft, and, especially with the Radpac incorporated, is one of the most formidable air-combat fighters now flying. But it is quite obvious that the same basic aircraft can be modified with a different radar, long-range air-to-air sensors, different avionics of various kinds, and different weapons in order to become an outstanding air-defence aircraft.

As outlined in the first chapter, the genesis of MRCA was marked by earnest arguments about just what species of animal the nations wanted. There is always a strong attraction to the 'small, simple, nimble, cheap fighter'. MRCA participants were often almost torn in two by the conflicting views, and two of them walked out when they saw the way the aircraft was crystallising. It had all happened before with the F-111, which finally jelled at gross weights between 92,500 and 114,300lb, and with so little 'fighter'

Left: Impression by Artist Derek Bunce of Tornado F2 killing two crossing targets at close range. In fact Sky Flash would normally be fired at ranges around 30 miles (48km), but then the artist could not have shown the targets! Even today some observers in the media proclaim that Tornado lacks thrust or manoeuvrability; they ignore the fact the RAF chose not to use uprated RB.199 engines and that F2 meets all the operational requirements./*BAe*

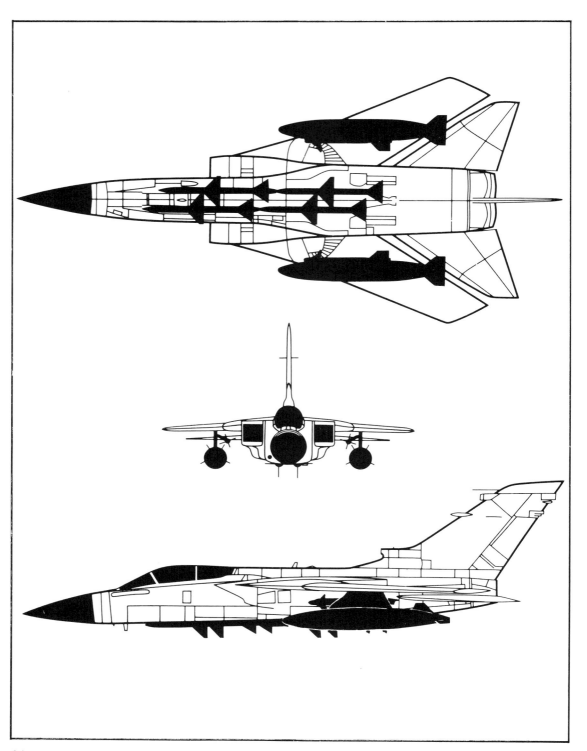

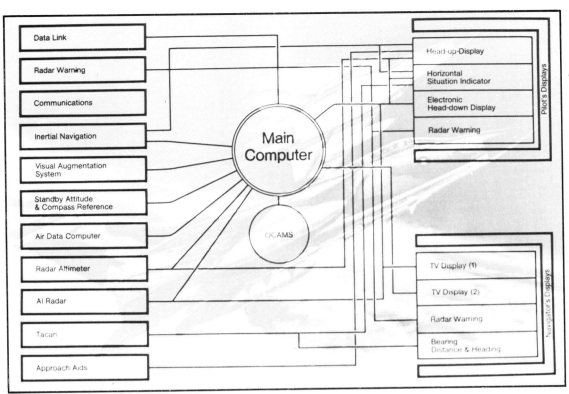

Data Link		Head-up-Display
Radar Warning		Horizontal Situation Indicator
Communications	Main Computer	Electronic Head-down Display
Inertial Navigation		Radar Warning
Visual Augmentation System		Pilot's Displays
Standby Attitude & Compass Reference		
Air Data Computer	OCAMS	
Radar Altimeter		TV Display (1)
AI Radar		TV Display (2)
Tacan		Radar Warning
Approach Aids		Bearing Distance & Heading
		Navigator's Displays

Left: Three-view of the Tornado F2, which has an almost wholly new forward fuselage; here it is depicted with four Sky Flash and two AIM-9L./*Panavia*

Above: Block diagram of the beautifully structured avionics system of the ADV, shown against a faint reproduction of another artist's impression./*BAe*

capability that I have yet to meet a One-Eleven jock who has ever fired the gun (which is seldom fitted). Europe did much better, and Tornado is scarcely half as heavy as an F-111, and very much more agile. Yet it is equipped with even better all-weather nav/attack systems, a heavy weapon load, and fuel for any mission it could possibly be tasked with. The 'small, simple, nimble, cheap fighter' would be unable to fly the missions, but would be excellent for airshows.

Now there are an infinite number of ways Tornado can be configured. The IDS version is the standard for the four initial customers, and a proportion are dual-control aircraft with well over 99 per cent commonality by value. Export customers can have Radpac, to give enhanced air-to-air capability, the commonality of the rest of the aircraft being 100%.

My own belief is that this cost/effective option will eventually be selected for the four initial customers also, because when matched with Sky Flash or Sparrow it turns the IDS into an even better fighter without penalty in other roles. But it is clearly possible to go much further along this path. At the far air-to-air end of the spectrum would be an aircraft with a large fixed wing and much bigger engines, rather like an F-15. This would be extremely costly to develop, much less versatile and merely a re-invention of an American product. On the way one would pass through an aircraft rather like the F-14 Tomcat, but the latter has a unique radar/missile combination which is extremely expensive but has unrivalled range and multiple-target capability. It would have been fairly straightforward, with the agreement of the US government and co-operation of Hughes Aircraft, to put the same radar/missile combination into an air-defence Tornado, but the cost would still have been daunting.

Though all the four initial Tornado customers are naturally interested in the air-to-air role, Britain's obligations are the greatest. The RAF is tasked with maintaining the integrity of the UK Air Defence Region. This is much bigger than NATO's Central Region, for it extends from Iceland to the Channel, and from the Atlantic Approaches to the Baltic. This obviously means that a fighter to protect this region must have long range (the mind boggles at how the Air Staff came to formulate the F.23/49 specification which gave the first Lightnings about enough fuel to guard one British county.) Endurance in the subsonic loiter mode is also important. It must be possible to engage targets flying at both very high altitudes and just above the Earth's surface, and from the greatest possible range. It must do so whilst in the presence of the most sophisticated ECM. Other requirements are rapid response from ground alert and a high aerodynamic performance, including combat manoeuvrability.

It is worth noting that, though these are the requirements for a UK Air Defence Region interceptor for use in possible time of conflict, unidentified military aircraft have for many years entered this region almost every day and have to be 'escorted off the premises'. Called 'Zombies', they are long-range Tu-95, Tu-16 or M-4 ocean-reconnaissance, Elint and missile-guidance platforms of the Soviet Union's ADD (long-range aviation) and AV-MF (naval aviation). The main objective is to test Britain's response and, as a by-product, record and analyse all the electromagnetic emissions that can be detected. This is a valid peacetime task for the Russians, and it is equally reasonable to respond to it; failure to do so might conceivably lead to dangerous political adventures. Today the Phantom has replaced the short-ranged but popular Lightning on the anti-Zombie run. Undoubtedly the Russian aircrew know exactly what a Phantom can do, and do not have to fly so close to RAF Leuchars in order to allow interception to take place. But even the Phantom was only adopted as an interim aircraft. Though it is capable, has good fuel capacity and no acute fatigue problem, it has always (ie from date of its purchase in 1966) been judged to need replacing in the RAF in the early to mid-1980s.

In fact the growing capability of Warsaw Pact aircraft has tended to move the date of replacement forward rather than back. When MRCA was in the planning stage in 1967-9 the RAF OR (Operational Requirements) branch first hit on the apparently excellent solution of producing MRCA as a replacement for both the Vulcan and Buccaneer in the strike/attack role and the Phantom in the air-defence role. This was a new idea – though AFVG had been planned as a replacement for Buccaneer, Lightning and Phantom – and one that would have been most unlikely had either the TSR.2 or F-111K been put into service, because these would have been much less suitable in the air-defence role. One recalls that the quest for commonality between the US Air Force attack F-111 and the Navy fighter F-111 proved a costly failure. With today's Tornado there is no difficulty – at least, none arising from the aircraft.

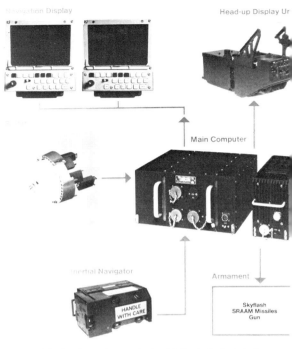

Above: Major hardware elements in the ADV avionics include the so-called Foxhunter radar by Marconi, with Ferranti's contribution including the inverse-Cassegrain aerial system; a main computer and HUD similar to those of the IDS; and two tab displays identical in design but with different labelling on the interface keys to suit the different needs of the mission./*Panavia*

Above right: Taken in May 1979, this photograph of the first F2 shows the aircraft structurally complete (indeed carrying four dummy Sky Flash) but lacking a few details and still in the yellow-ochre primer finish. It was to fly later in 1979, in an odd white and grey paint scheme./*BAe*

Right: This close-up of the first ADV, prior to painting, shows the muzzle of the single MK27 gun and the way the forward pair of Sky Flash medium-range AAMs are recessed while the rear pair have only wings and fins recessed./*BAe*

What became called the ADV (Air-Defence Variant) emerged in 1969, though it took several further years of refinement before it was made public. At that time there was no apparent need for hurry; in fact one of the problems was that the RAF did not want the ADV (it thought) until the mid-1980s, after the IDS force was expected to have been built. Today the picture has – and I am tempted to add 'predictably' – changed. The Soviet threat has sharpened and intensified, as it was bound to do, while Panavia has unfortunately suffered slippage on the ADV if anything

worse than on the IDS Tornado. In retrospect it seems unfortunate that the ADV was started so long after the IDS programme, in such an unhurried atmosphere. As it is at present a UK-only aircraft, that country is paying the whole cost of development, and the ADV price reflects its smaller production run.

How the programme began has been outlined by Group Captain John Fraser, DDOR 3 (RAF) at the Ministry of Defence: 'We defined the ADV by the time-honoured method of evaluating the threat and then deciding on the characteristics of an aircraft to counter it. In this case we considered that, in the event of hostilities involving NATO and the WP countries, the prime threat to the UK would likely be from low-level relatively highspeed bombers of the Backfire and Fencer types with, perhaps, some Foxbat reconnaissance support: multiple target formations under extensive ECM cover would be a likely mode of attack. Bearing in mind the additional task of providing air-defence cover for our maritime forces and the need to meet the high- and medium-level supersonic threat, it is readily apparent that our requirement is for a long-range multi-purpose interceptor rather than the much narrower potential offered by an air-superiority fighter.

'Obviously it was necessary to evaluate the alternatives. The main contenders have been examined in some detail ... The F-16 lacks the fundamental all-weather capability we need ... The F-15, though a good Central Region fighter, is a single-seat aircraft with only a limited radar and ECCM capability; we would have had largely to re-equip it to make it suitable for our role. The F-14, which would have broadly met our needs, was, and still is, far too expensive and had to be discarded at a very early stage in our deliberations.' He concluded his review, 'The Tornado F2 not only fulfils our requirement supremely well but enables us to capitalise on the considerable investment we have made in the MRCA programme. Together with its sister-ship, the GR1, the RAF is getting a first-class combat aircraft in Tornado that we believe will satisfy our strike/attack and air-defence needs until the turn of the century.'

Despite the slippage, the first F2 should have flown well before this book appears. It looks pretty much like other Tornados, though the nose is slimmer and more pointed. In fact, though overall commonality by cost is officially put at 80%, the front end of the interceptor

Right: Roll-out of the first Tornado F2, with the VCAS, Air Marshal Sir John Nicholls, at the microphone. He said it was 'by far the best to do the job we have to do'. On the same day he flew IDS Tornado P.03./*BAe*

has been redesigned. The radar is completely new, and naturally designed specifically for this challenging application. The radome is longer and has a smaller cone semi-angle giving higher speeds. Avionics generally are unchanged, but there are numerous detail revisions, completely altered system configuration, and wholly different software. The ECM/ECCM are totally new, and include an impressive modular RHAW (radar homing and warning) receiver. The cockpit displays are modified, the combined radar/map displays and pilot's TF display disappearing and being replaced by a new electronic HDD (head-down display) and augmented radar-warning and other displays. The pilot's HUD combiner glass gives deeper field of view. A vital addition is a VAS (visual augmentation system) for detecting and positively identifying targets far beyond normal visual range. Main armament comprises four Sky Flash MRAAMs (medium-range air-to-air missiles) recessed under the fuselage in staggered pairs. To accommodate these nose-to-tail the fuselage has been slightly lengthened aft of the cockpits, and this neatly accommodates another 200 Imp gal of fuel. Unlike the IDS the FR probe is a permanent fit and it retracts fully on the left side, not the right. The fixed wing glove is extended forward in the usual way on modern fighters to generate vortex lift at high angles of attack, and Krüger flaps are not fitted. The left gun is removed, providing space for additional avionics. The last point that should be emphasized in this brief list is that, after the ADV had been aerodynamically refined to reduce drag, no extra thrust was needed. In fact it is certain that more powerful engines will become available before deliveries of the Tornado F2 begin several years hence, but these will be a bonus. The oft-repeated suggestion that more power is a necessity is incorrect.

I will now quickly run through the chief parts of the ADV system in more detail. Marconi-Elliott Avionics produce the radar, with Ferranti handling the transmitter and aerial scanner; and the resulting set, unofficially dubbed Foxhunter, is the most advanced ever created in Europe, and in most respects better than any US interception radar (comparisons are odious, and the American AWG-9, though much

older, and the APG-63 and -65 score in some ways and are inferior in others). Suffice to say, in my opinion nothing will beat this radar in its operational role against heavy jamming by clever enemies. Of course, no TFR is fitted.

Foxhunter is a high-prf pulse-doppler with an unusual twist-reflecting Cassegrain aerial driven hydraulically. This gives very accurate pointing, small sidelobes and good performance against sea-level targets using ECM. It also does well in air-ground mapping and ranging, as demonstrated since 1975 in a Canberra, but its prime purpose is to detect targets at distances up to 100 nautical miles (115 miles), track them automatically and feed their trajectory parameters continuously to the main computer and the displays, in this version for the pilot as well as the navigator. It naturally uses digital microelectronics for signal and data processing, and according to *Flight International* operates in I/J band. Normally operating with both crew, with or without UKADGE or Nimrod AEW data-links, it clearly handles multiple targets and can provide target illumination for Sky Flash guidance; how many targets can be handled has not been disclosed, but the TWS (track while scan) and computer handling of data are designed for single interceptors to take on mass raids. The crew need to know the positive identity of targets, the sequence in which they should be engaged, how the aircraft should be steered and much more. All this is presented clearly. I need not repeat here the numerous advantages of Sky Flash over the AIM-7E from which it was derived (or, except in the matter of range, AIM-7F). Should the Tornado find itself in close contact with the enemy the pilot can instantly take control of the radar for snap acquisition and quick firing of AIM-9L Sidewinder or the gun.

The next, splendidly vivid contribution comes from Wing Commander Mike Elsam, of DOR (1) at Ministry of Defence (RAF): 'I'll start by summarising how we intend to solve the target-identification problem. There is no single solution, so we believe in the use of a number of sensors. Obviously the radar will help us find our target and analyse its behaviour. A Mach 2.5, 60,000ft response heading towards the UK is unlikely to be a friend! Secondly, we will have an on-line netted data ECM-resistant data-link system. This will provide jam-resistant digital data transfer, secure speech and precise navigation information. The AEW Nimrod, some ships and the UKADGE will be in the data-link community, as well as the USAF and USN. The ADV will also be fitted with an integrated IFF interrogator.

'Next comes the VAS (visual augmentation system), which is a built-in EO (electro-optical) device displaying a TV picture of the target giving positive identification by day in good time for a front-

Above: During its first week of flying from BAe's Warton aerodrome in Lancashire, the first prototype of the Tornado Air Defence Variant (shown here with its wings swept at 45°, the combat setting) totalled 8¼ hours flying time, achieved Mach 1.75 and made a night landing. The pilot on the first and some of the subsequent flights, Warton Division's Chief Test Pilot, David Eagles, had these comments to make: 'One of the big plus points that have emerged so far is the improvement in supersonic acceleration because of the extra fuselage length and consequent fineness ratio. This is a most important operational consideration when accelerating to intercept a target.'/*BAe*

hemisphere firing and in starlight-only night conditions at ranges well in excess of what we need for safe shadowing and missile release. Finally we have a radar-warning receiver (RWR) which will be more like an electronic surveillance system. It will have a computer which will analyse detected emitters and provide a readout of what it thinks the target-type is and which direction it is coming from. Genuine threats to the aircraft, from SAMs, AI radars and similar sources, override any other selection and give audio as well as visual warnings.

'Let us now consider the type of displays the crew will have to utilise all this capability. The navigator will have two TV tabs on which he can call up several different formats. His basic working display is a range/azimuth picture incorporating TWS (track while scan). The radar can track a lot of targets at once whilst the computer provides precise flight data on any of them. In addition to this display there are two types of pulse, raw velocity, ground mapping, navigation and fixing, and fault-readout formats.

'The pilot will have a HUD and a single TV monitor beneath it. On his new TV tab he can have a duplicate of one of the displays in the rear cockpit, or he can call up his own attack display known as Lance – which, you will no doubt be enthralled to know, stands for line algorithm for navigation in a combat environment.

It provides all the information necessary for a missile attack, and is available once a particular target has been nominated. An attack can be completed on this display, but the pilot's main attack reference is the HUD. This is an advanced fixed-combiner system with a large field of view. The hardware is common to all Tornados, but the F2 symbology has been specially designed for the air-defence role. Incidentally this is the first time the RAF has had a HUD in its interceptors, and we feel it will considerably enhance our combat effectiveness. We hope, in the not-too-distant future, to have a helmet-mounted sight to supplement the HUD, and our F2 avionics have been designed to cater for this eventuality.

'There is one other display which we think is pretty revolutionary. It's our Tactical Planning Format, on which the crew will do all their threat-analysis, evaluate alternative attack sequences, and decide on the best weapon options. The picture is a north-orientated plan view on which CAP points, MEZs, AEW barriers and all other locations can be shown, as well as all the targets and co-operating fighters.

'I don't want to give the impression that the computer controls all – it doesn't. We have deliberately designed the system so that the processors do the number-crunching and the crew decide what action to take. In other words the computers are advisory, and in no way executive. As well as these "normal" modes of weapon and attack selection, we have a pilot overriding system which enables him to enter a visual fight controlling all the weapons without taking his hand off the stick and throttles. So, overall, we have a very flexible setup of displays and controls, ranging from the computer-assisted long-range evaluation to the close-in visual fight.'

Elsam's bubbling enthusiasm is shared by everyone else involved with the Tornado F2. People who know nothing about it, such as the media, have looked for something to criticise and have decided the aircraft can't be any good because it has too little wing area and too little thrust. Even *Flight International,* which ought to know better, has written of its 'poor manoeuvrability when compared with US and Soviet dogfighting aircraft', and rated it poorly in a major review of air-combat fighters simply because when plotted on a graph of wing loading and thrust/weight ratio it appeared to come in the wrong place. The magazine's review concluded that a better choice for the world's air forces might be the American F-18, supposedly smaller, simpler and cheaper than the 'heavyweights' such as the F-15 and Tornado. For the record, the F-18 is in most respects larger than the European aircraft, it is simpler only to the extent that it suffers a fixed wing, it is slower, and it is extremely unlikely to be cheaper (no meaningful 'price' can be quoted, but the 15 ordered by the US Navy in 1979 are priced at $1,044 million).

Nobody would pretend that an RAF crew could take-off in an F2 with maximum fuel and weapons and tangle with an F-16. It is as outclassed in such an 'eyeball' match as the F-16 would be trying to do the Tornado F2's tasks hundreds of miles out over the Atlantic on a winter's night. Nobody can have everything in one aircraft, and the RAF have little need for the close-combat visual fighter which has unfortunately dominated the thinking of so many air forces. Its true need is for a fighter able to check on everything that enters gigantic blocks of airspace, identify it precisely and quickly, and if necessary destroy it from a distance. The only really weak link in the Tornado F2 chain, in my view, is the need to fly towards every target to illuminate it while the Sky Flash is in flight. This necessity has been demonstrated time and again – with the F-4, F-14 and F-15 – to be stupidly dangerous, because it inevitably brings the interceptor close to the target which, at the last moment, can destroy the interceptor with a short-range 'launch and leave' IR missile. As long as we use semi-active radar homing missiles we shall have to resign ourselves to the pointless game of swapping aircraft one-for-one (unless we can put the target-illuminating radar in the tail or laterally so that the range need not be closed). Apart from this problem, which the Americans hope to overcome with the AMRAAM (Sparrow replacement) by making this new missile a self-homer, the Tornado F2 appears an ideal aircraft in all respects for any nation with a fair amount of real estate to protect. Air-combat manoeuvrability is not particularly important for it, but turn radius is nothing to be ashamed of and rather better than that of the Lightning and Phantom. In Mike Elsam's words, compared with the Phantom, 'It accelerates better, is a good bit faster, and has far better handling qualities, particularly at low speeds.

It can go twice as far or stay airborne twice as long on the same fuel. Range is certainly not a problem; its ferry range will get us from the UK to Cyprus nonstop without refuelling, whilst carrying a full missile load'.

I have been impressed by the public statements made on the Tornado F2 by Ministers and officials because they demonstrate a welcome improvement both in future planning and a more 'open' style of government. The need for it has been carefully spelt out, and the operational and financial evaluations against possible foreign candidate aircraft a most desirable innovation. Full-scale development was authorised on 4 March 1976, and the initial production contract for 40 Tornados was adjusted and priced to comprise 37 IDS and three ADV. These three aircraft are now recognisable, and the intention is that of the total run of 809 production machines 165 will be ADVs, designated F2 by the RAF. Though this version causes slightly more of a hiccup than the two-pilot IDS version, especially to British Aerospace which builds the front end, it is infinitely simpler both from the industrial and RAF points of view than having a different type of aircraft. And both Germany and Italy have a very keen eye on this version because during the 1980s both will need a long-range allweather interceptor in this class, the Luftwaffe's as an F-4 replacement.

Predictably, the media have devoted great attention to the suggestion that the ADV might be cancelled. This appears to stem mainly from the belief that, as a one-nation programme, it is more vulnerable than the basic IDS version. In fact there is a bit more to it than this. First, cancellation would rob Germany of 165 sets of centre fuselages and Italy of 165 sets of wings, and Turbo-Union of more than 400 engines. Second, there is no visible aircraft that could so economically meet the requirement. One of the popular tales has been that, in return for a USAF buy of IDS Tornado, Britain would buy the F-15 instead of the ADV, though this suggestion runs contrary to everything said by all the people in a position to take decisions. Another 'replacement' someone found attractive is little-used ex-Iranian F-14s. Yet a further spurt to such daydreaming was provided by the statement of the Under-Secretary of State for Air on 27 March 1979 that 'The Air Force has given careful consideration to the possibility of increasing the number of air-defence fighters available to the UK. A decision has been taken in principle'. I think this merely meant that, if the Saudis agree to a Lightning life-extension programme, British Aerospace can remanufacture enough to form another stop-gap RAF squadron. And it would be extraordinary if, over the next 15 years, the ADV did not commend itself to at least eight customers outside the original Panavia partnership.

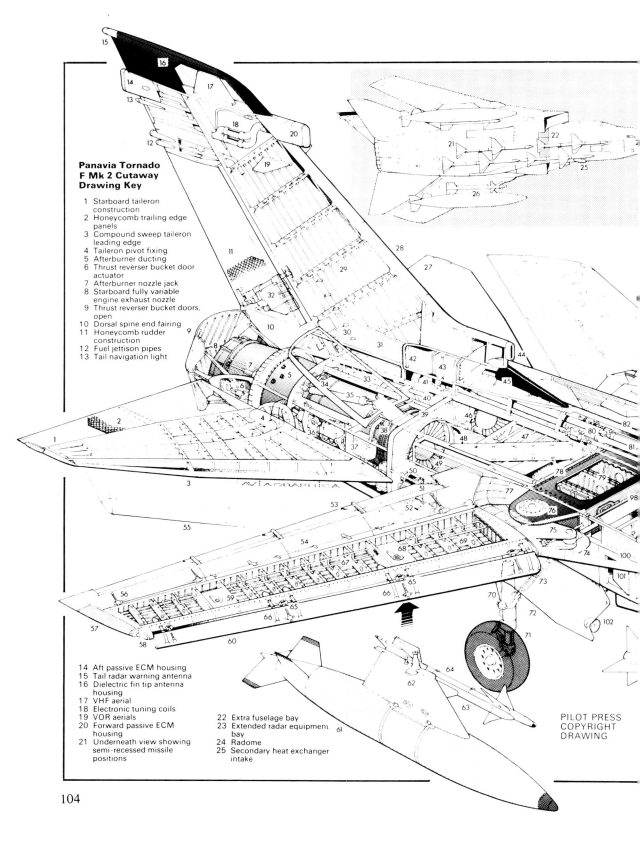

Panavia Tornado
F Mk 2 Cutaway
Drawing Key

1 Starboard taileron
  construction
2 Honeycomb trailing edge
  panels
3 Compound sweep taileron
  leading edge
4 Taileron pivot fixing
5 Afterburner ducting
6 Thrust reverser bucket door
  actuator
7 Afterburner nozzle jack
8 Starboard fully variable
  engine exhaust nozzle
9 Thrust reverser bucket doors,
  open
10 Dorsal spine end fairing
11 Honeycomb rudder
   construction
12 Fuel jettison pipes
13 Tail navigation light

14 Aft passive ECM housing
15 Tail radar warning antenna
16 Dielectric fin tip antenna
   housing
17 VHF aerial
18 Electronic tuning coils
19 VOR aerials
20 Forward passive ECM
   housing
21 Underneath view showing
   semi-recessed missile
   positions

22 Extra fuselage bay
23 Extended radar equipment
   bay
24 Radome
25 Secondary heat exchanger
   intake

PILOT PRESS
COPYRIGHT
DRAWING

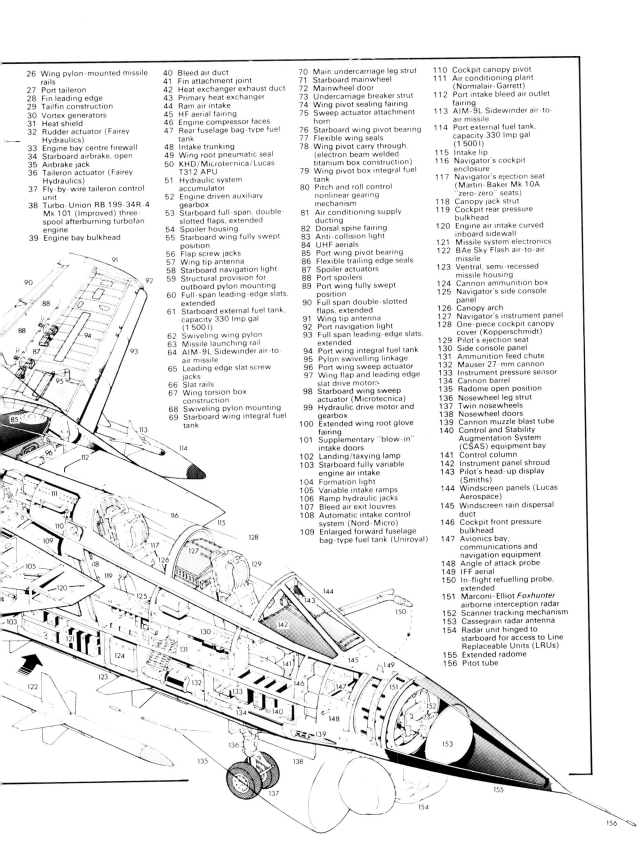

26 Wing pylon-mounted missile rails
27 Port taileron
28 Fin leading edge
29 Tailfin construction
30 Vortex generators
31 Heat shield
32 Rudder actuator (Fairey Hydraulics)
33 Engine bay centre firewall
34 Starboard airbrake, open
35 Airbrake jack
36 Taileron actuator (Fairey Hydraulics)
37 Fly-by-wire taileron control unit
38 Turbo-Union RB.199-34R-4 Mk 101 (Improved) three-spool afterburning turbofan engine
39 Engine bay bulkhead
40 Bleed air duct
41 Fin attachment joint
42 Heat exchanger exhaust duct
43 Primary heat exchanger
44 Ram air intake
45 HF aerial fairing
46 Engine compressor faces
47 Rear fuselage bag-type fuel tank
48 Intake trunking
49 Wing root pneumatic seal
50 KHD/Microtecnica/Lucas T312 APU
51 Hydraulic system accumulator
52 Engine driven auxiliary gearbox
53 Starboard full-span, double-slotted flaps, extended
54 Spoiler housing
55 Starboard wing fully swept position
56 Flap screw jacks
57 Wing tip antenna
58 Starboard navigation light
59 Structural provision for outboard pylon mounting
60 Full-span leading-edge slats, extended
61 Starboard external fuel tank, capacity 330 Imp gal (1 500 l)
62 Swiveling wing pylon
63 Missile launching rail
64 AIM-9L Sidewinder air-to-air missile
65 Leading edge slat screw jacks
66 Slat rails
67 Wing torsion box construction
68 Swiveling pylon mounting
69 Starboard wing integral fuel tank
70 Main undercarriage leg strut
71 Starboard mainwheel
72 Mainwheel door
73 Undercarriage breaker strut
74 Wing pivot sealing fairing
75 Sweep actuator attachment horn
76 Starboard wing pivot bearing
77 Flexible wing seals
78 Wing pivot carry through, (electron beam welded titanium box construction)
79 Wing pivot box integral fuel tank
80 Pitch and roll control nonlinear gearing mechanism
81 Air conditioning supply ducting
82 Dorsal spine fairing
83 Anti-collision light
84 UHF aerials
85 Port wing pivot bearing
86 Flexible trailing edge seals
87 Spoiler actuators
88 Port spoilers
89 Port wing fully swept position
90 Full span double-slotted flaps, extended
91 Wing tip antenna
92 Port navigation light
93 Full span leading-edge slats, extended
94 Port wing integral fuel tank
95 Pylon swivelling linkage
96 Port wing sweep actuator
97 Wing flap and leading edge slat drive motors
98 Starboard wing sweep actuator (Microtecnica)
99 Hydraulic drive motor and gearbox
100 Extended wing root glove fairing
101 Supplementary "blow-in" intake doors
102 Landing/taxying lamp
103 Starboard fully variable engine air intake
104 Formation light
105 Variable intake ramps
106 Ramp hydraulic jacks
107 Bleed air exit louvres
108 Automatic intake control system (Nord-Micro)
109 Enlarged forward fuselage bag-type fuel tank (Uniroyal)
110 Cockpit canopy pivot
111 Air conditioning plant (Normalair-Garrett)
112 Port intake bleed air outlet fairing
113 AIM-9L Sidewinder air-to-air missile
114 Port external fuel tank, capacity 330 Imp gal (1 500 l)
115 Intake lip
116 Navigator's cockpit enclosure
117 Navigator's ejection seat (Martin-Baker Mk 10A "zero-zero" seats)
118 Canopy jack strut
119 Cockpit rear pressure bulkhead
120 Engine air intake curved inboard sidewall
121 Missile system electronics
122 BAe Sky Flash air-to-air missile
123 Ventral, semi-recessed missile housing
124 Cannon ammunition box
125 Navigator's side console panel
126 Canopy arch
127 Navigator's instrument panel
128 One-piece cockpit canopy cover (Kopperschmidt)
129 Pilot's ejection seat
130 Side console panel
131 Ammunition feed chute
132 Mauser 27-mm cannon
133 Instrument pressure sensor
134 Cannon barrel
135 Radome open position
136 Nosewheel leg strut
137 Twin nosewheels
138 Nosewheel doors
139 Cannon muzzle blast tube
140 Control and Stability Augmentation System (CSAS) equipment bay
141 Control column
142 Instrument panel shroud
143 Pilot's head-up display (Smiths)
144 Windscreen panels (Lucas Aerospace)
145 Windscreen rain dispersal duct
146 Cockpit front pressure bulkhead
147 Avionics bay, communications and navigation equipment
148 Angle of attack probe
149 IFF aerial
150 In-flight refuelling probe, extended
151 Marconi-Elliot *Foxhunter* airborne interception radar
152 Scanner tracking mechanism
153 Cassegrain radar antenna
154 Radar unit hinged to starboard for access to Line Replaceable Units (LRUs)
155 Extended radome
156 Pitot tube

An Overview

Bearing in mind the rapidity with which the butterfly-like minds of Air Staffs have sometimes changed Operational Requirements, so that hardware to meet the requirement was delayed or even cancelled, it is little short of a miracle that we should today have Tornados coming off the production line looking almost exactly like the aircraft planned ten years ago. It is rather as if the Battle of Britain had been fought by aircraft designed in the 1920s, but we are not really entering an era of technical stagnation. Skyhawk, Comet/Nimrod, Harrier and B-52 are examples of other aircraft programmes that will span a half-century, but things happen to them every day of the week as they progress toward maturity.

An obvious question for an overview is 'Why ten years?' My own view is that, with the notable exception of Jaguar, collaborative programmes take longer, often by 100 or more per cent. Alpha Jet is a prime example of a project which, had it been a national one like the rival Hawk, might have proceeded at twice the pace. The reason has been an army of officials, all eager to keep the project properly managed. Indeed, many of the delays — and I am writing of Tornado especially — have been due to the refusal of the officials to sanction release pending further detailed studies to show how cost can be minimised. In an inflationary environment this automatically wastes not only time but also money.

Europe has a bad record of not adhering to estimated costs in its advanced weapon systems, and with prolonged delays the objective becomes impossible. In this area Tornado has done outstandingly well. Despite the media, who appear unable to compare the costs of Tornado with those of broadly similar US programmes such as the F-14, F-15 and F-18, Tornado is very far from being 'expensive' if by that adjective is meant costly by comparison with its rivals. In terms of the programme currency unit, the 1970 Deutschmark, there has been no escalation in price whatever. Manhours per airframe have held level and some material costs have actually fallen. The only real problem with pricing and the wish to avoid money crossing frontiers has been the soaring value of the real DM, so that Germany's partners have been hard pressed to make a real profit. At the start of the programme in 1969 the exchange rate was 12.2 DM to £1, but by 1974 the figure had been halved; for a time Panavia operated on an 'official' rate of 8.7, later reduced to 7, but even these ratios did not reflect the actual value of the German currency.

Bearing in mind factors of this kind, and the sheer impossibility of calculating R&D costs — for example, why charge Tornado with the whole, and extremely large, R&D cost of a new engine and gun which are to be used in other programmes? — the following are some of the public statements made on Tornado costs:

October 1973, UK: 'The estimated unit cost of MRCA at 1970 values, excluding R&D, is £1.7 million.'

May 1974, FRG: 'The commonly accepted unit price is DM 20 million' (FRG prices are exclusive of R&D).

November 1974, UK: 'The total cost of development to the beginning of September (1974) was £345 million. The UK's share of this is £116 million, of which the major part has been paid in sterling in the UK, compared with an estimated £114 million in 1970. Of this increase, £40 million is due to inflation, £2 million to devaluation of sterling against DM, and £8 million to increase in the UK share of work following FRG's reduction in planned requirement from 420 to 322'.

February 1975, UK: 'Estimated unit cost of the common (IDS) version, inclusive of R&D, is £3.9 million at September 1974 levels'.

January 1976, UK: 'The unit cost of the IDS Tornado is £5.29 million at economic conditions and exchange rates applicable to 1976-77 estimates'.

April 1976, FRG: 'Total cost of the 322 aircraft amounts to 15.5 billion DM at the December 1975 level' (excluding R&D).

May 1976, FRG: 'Though the production investment represents an overall commitment of 2,000 million DM, the unit cost is still only 25 million DM'.

December 1976, Italy: 'It can be stated that unit cost is 8.42 billion lire, and that the total spent on R&D by all partners has been 162 billion lire.'

Above right: This photograph captions itself; Ivan R. Yates, Warton Division managing director, is addressing the assembly. BT.001 made its maiden flight on 10 July, pilot Eagles commenting 'The standard was exceptionally high for a first production aircraft . . .'. /BAe

Right: The day after the roll-out of BT.001 this parallel ceremony was held at MBB Manching for the second production machine. /MBB

Above: Gen (ret) Limburg, former Luftwaffe Chief, makes sure all the parts have been put into GT.001, watched by Gero Madelung. */MBB*

June 1979, UK: Latest cost estimates published at £9 million for IDS and £10.98 million for ADV, presumably in 1979 sterling; CAS Sir Michael Beetham added '(these) sound like large figures but I would ask you to compare them with the cost of other aircraft that are around – you will find that Tornado is a remarkably good bargain'.

If these statements leave the reader confused, it must be borne in mind that they were the best the officials could do at the time. The apparent cost increase in Britain has been due to the falling value of sterling, more than any other factor. Asking the price of a Tornado is little better than asking 'How long is a piece of string?' Anyone who really wants to find out has to spend some time thinking the problem through. For example the above unit prices are for median aircraft, those delivered mid-way through the programme. Earlier ones will be cheaper and later ones more expensive. How the three currencies will relate when the 805th production aircraft is delivered a decade hence is impossible to guess, but unless there is severe decline in industrial performance in one of the partners there is a fair chance that Tornado will always be a 'better buy' than anything else offering similar capability, when such an aircraft comes along. There is no rival at present.

At the risk of appearing facetious I could comment that Jaguar was developed so fast and so cheaply because the engineers were allowed to do it in peace. In modern programme parlance, the 'visibility' was near-zero. 'Visibility' is a Pentagon expression

meaning that the customer, in America's case the Department of Defense, interfaces at all levels with the contractors to keep tabs on progress. With Tornado the American-derived rules on 'visibility' almost reached epidemic proportions, so that everyone working on Tornado was spending the working day explaining things to NAMMA and the customer air forces, filling in paperwork, delivering computer outputs and generally keeping very busy on everything except making Tornado. This was one of the major reasons for the protracted development and consequent inflation-induced rise in costs. Nobody suggests that vast military projects should proceed behind locked doors, but in my view the costs of high visibility in the Tornado programme have been at a level which taxpayers ought to consider unacceptable.

If the nations of Western Europe had strong political will, a stronger wish for commonality and inter-operability and a total absence of government based on short-term expediency and party-political gain, it would not be long before NATO had some real muscle and the media viewed European (especially British) aircraft as probably sensible and likely to be produced in large numbers. As it is, even the Treasury in Whitehall loses no opportunity of trying to prove that it would be better to cancel everything, while the Select Committee on Estimates sees it as its function to promote the adoption of foreign aircraft that may not do the job but which appear to be 'cheaper'. Not even Tornado's outstanding technical success cuts much ice against the destructive built-in headwinds in the European environment.

A second cause for concern is the loss of substantial numbers of experienced engineers from the British industry, most of them to jobs in North America, because of a progressive worsening of their position in the national scale of pay – which in any case, in their opinion at least, compares unfavourably with other countries. This has hit British Aerospace at a time when its technical work-load has been rising sharply, and part of the result is a continuing slippage in Tornado accomplishments. In the case of ADV this slippage, combined with the endemic uncertainty that has bedevilled British programmes, appears to be reinforcing political moves to adopt some foreign solution in order to get more fighters sooner, even if that means throwing the RAF into disarray and running the country into very large costs spread over the next 30 years. This may sound a slightly shrill outburst, but that is the message that appeared to come from the House of Commons statement of 27 March 1979. One really thought we had moved beyond such short-sighted policy, and I shall be relieved if all the statement actually meant was refurbishing of some of the Lightnings then in storage for a brief spell of re-use.

It does not seem long since the first Lightnings entered service with No 74 Squadron at Coltishall (in fact it is 20 years), but though these introduced a considerably higher level of performance than the preceding generation (the Hunter) the pilot's job could have been mastered by any wartime fighter pilot after an hour or two of reading. The Tornado, on the other hand, is a new generation of technology even for anyone brought up on today's hardware such as the Phantom or F-104G. As far as flying is concerned the Tornado is a marvellous improvement, with none of the fierce, tricky or dangerous features of earlier tactical aircraft, and a wholly new level of ride comfort in extreme low-level turbulence. But where the serious flying of missions is concerned the aircrew have to learn a new way of operating, interfacing with their intelligent aircraft via video displays and computers. In a way it is not all that different from 1940, when the first radar operators in night fighters tried to derive sense from the spiky 'grass' on small cathode-ray tubes. But the validity of the problem is shown by the probability that, despite my attempt to make it simple, parts of this book have probably gone clean over the heads of many readers. (At the same time, it may have triggered a spark of excitement in some, and set them on the long road that leads to a Tornado squadron, which is a fine man-size job.)

Hopefully we in Europe will never lack the people we need to build and fly Tornado. This has been officially called 'unquestionably the most important military venture at present being undertaken in Europe'. At the political, industrial and military levels it has done more than anything other than the formation of NATO itself to unify Europe, strengthen the alliance of Western democracies and generally bring so-called 'foreign' people together in a common cause. It is part of the price we pay for freedom that we tend to distrust each other and read into statements or actions motives that were not intended. Though there are still a sprinkling of narrow small-minded nationalists left in Europe, most people today have a wider and better-informed view, and nothing has done more to bring this about than Tornado. It took about a year, say 1969-70, for lingering feelings of suspicion to be dissipated; since then the team that has grown to be the biggest in the world has worked with an almost complete absence of friction — less than in a national programme — to solve the technical problems.

In collaboration one of the areas that dies hardest is the wish to preserve commercial advantage. The transfer of ultra-new technology and company secrets to so-called 'foreign rivals' is something nobody learns easily, and in working out how to avoid this being a stumbling-block European aerospace companies lead the rest of the world by miles.

As I write, the US Under-Secretary of Defense for Research and Engineering has just announced 'We will be especially attentive to transfer of technology that could reduce our industrial competitive edge . . .' He says that, though Europe has adopted the F-16, its F100 engine and the AIM-9L Sidewinder missile, numerous parts of all three will not be permitted to be made in Europe but will be supplied from the United States. In the same statement it was announced that, notwithstanding the existence of Britain's Sky Flash, it is proposed that the as-yet non-existent AMRAAM has been proposed as the future standard medium-range missile for NATO, and that technical information on Tornado has been requested by the Pentagon 'to check the compatibility of the AMRAAM candidate missiles'. Is one's correct response one of suspicion at this attempt to find out about Europe's most advanced aircraft (which undoubtedly poses a threat to US industry) and kill off the best existing air-to-air missile in the West? Or are we all on the same side?

In the past the United States has shown little understanding of how a collaborative programme works. Once or twice it has — magnanimously, as to a small-town cousin — adopted an item developed in Europe; more often it has sold Europe one of its own creations in a large international deal. But an international collaborative aerospace programme, such as Concorde, Transall, Atlantic, Jaguar, Alpha Jet, Roland, Hot, Milan or, above all, Tornado, has never even been attempted, except for a tank, that proved a disaster. But such a thing is not impossible. Even the F-18 Hornet is a collaborative programme, because McDonnell Douglas and Northrop are by no means the same company; but this is not quite the same as linking three nations. In a perilous world, collaborative defence could prove vital. Europe can feel very proud indeed of what it has accomplished in international collaboration, and of Tornado in particular.

Appendices

Tornado IDS Specification

Span: at 25° 45ft 7.25in (13.9m); at 68° 28ft 2.5in (8.6m)
Length: 54ft 9.5in (16.7m)
Height: 18ft 8.5in (5.7m)
Taileron span: 22ft 3.5in (6.8m)
Track: 10ft 2in (3.1m)
Wheelbase: 20ft 4in (6.2m)
Weight: approx 23,000lb (10,450kg) empty, equipped; over 40,000lb (18,140kg) clean, with full internal fuel; just under 60,000lb (27,200kg) max with full weapon load
Engines: Two Turbo-Union RB.199-34R Mk 101 three-shaft afterburning turbo fans with integral reversers:
Max diameter 34.25in (870mm)
Length overall 126in (3.2m)
Dry weight under 2,000lb (900kg)
Mass airflow 154lb/sec (70kg/sec)
Pressure ratio over 23:1
Max static thrust over 8,000lb (35kN) dry, over 15,000lb (66kN) with full afterburner

Avionics: *Communications* Plessey PTR.1721 (UK, Italy) or Rohde und Schwarz (Germany) uhf/vhf; AEG-Telefunken uhf/DF (UK, Germany); Chelton uhf homer aerial; SIT/Siemens emergency uhf with Rohde und Schwarz switch; BAe hf/SSB aerial tuning unit; Rohde und Schwarz (UK, Germany) or Montedel (Italy) hf/SSB radio; Ultra communications control system; Marconi Avionics central suppression unit; Epsilon voice recorder; Chelton com/ILS aerials.
Nav/attack Texas Instruments main and TFR radars; Ferranti DINS and combined radar/map displays; Decca Type 72 doppler; Microtecnica air-data computer; Litef Spirit 3 16-bit central computer; Aeritalia radio altimeter; Smiths/Teldix/OMI electronic HUD with Davall camera; Ferranti LRMTR laser; Marconi Avionics/AEG/Selenia TV tab displays; Astronautics (US) bearing/distance/heading indicator and contour-map display.

Defensive Siemens (Germany) or Cossor SSR-3100 (UK) IFF transponder; Elettronica EL-73 radar warning system; MSDS/Plessey/Decca passive ECM system; active ECM also carried. Study of photographs shows that on the fin are mounted front and rear aerials outwardly resembling those of the familiar ARI.18228 radar warning receiver system produced by MSDS and used on the two-seat Buccaneer and Phantom FGR2. On the outermost wing pylons Tornados have often carried the old Westinghouse ALQ-101(V) widely used by NATO air forces, the version most commonly seen being the (V)8 with TWT power and both fore and aft deception and jamming modes. British and German Tornados have been seen with another EW pod on this pylon, with twin anhedralled tail fins and a small ventral ram inlet; this appears to be a version of the ARI.23246 Ajax active/passive multi-threat ECM pod produced by a consortium led by MSDS and said unofficially to operate in I/J bands. Italian and German Tornados have often carried another ECM pod with no ventral inlet but with four square aerial windows on each side; this has not been publicly identified. American sources add the BAe CIMS ECM internal power-management system, a BAe EO pod, the Marconi AD.980 ECM central suppression processor unit and (Germany only) BOZ-10 chaff dispenser pod.

Weapons:
Standard fit includes two IWKA-Mauser 27mm cannon, specially developed for this aircraft, with extremely high muzzle velocity and two selectable rates of fire. No detailed schedule of weapons and external pylon/hardpoint ratings has been published, but the standard attachment is the Sandall/MACE 14 in ejector-release (ER) unit, and a Marconi Avionics/Selenia stores-management system is fitted. On long-range missions the two inboard pylons on the swing wings (which are especially deep so that stores clear the tailerons) would carry 330 Imp gal (1,500 litre) drop tanks. These pylons also have side rails for AIM-9L Sidewinder or other close-range missiles. Bomb loads of at least 10,000lb (4,540kg) can be carried along the two rows of ER units on the fuselage. EW or other pods can be carried on the swivelling outer-wing pylons (the inner wing pylons also swivel and can be fully loaded at 68° sweep with speed greater than Mach 1). The list of weapons for which IDS Tornado is cleared includes the following: virtually all free-fall tactical bombs of the RAF, Luftwaffe, Marineflieger, AMI and US Air Force and Navy, including practice bombs, cluster bombs, the MW-1 dispenser of bomblets, napalm, chemical stores, Lepus and other flare bombs, at least five types of retarded bombs; all available rocket pods; AS.30, AJ.168/AS.37 Martel, JP.233, Kormoran, Jumbo, Maverick, P3T cruise

Martel, and Hobos and Paveway 'smart' weapons; and AIM-9B, 9L and other Sidewinders, AIM-7E, 7E2 and 7F Sparrows, Sky Flash, and Aspide 1A.

Above: Fitted with the FR probe, 03 is seen here engaged in fully armed operational readiness trials from a hardened shelter at RAF Bentwaters, a USAF base in Essex; at the same time in June 1978 a German Tornado was in a shelter at MFG Schleswig./*BAe*

Performance

Maximum demonstrated Mach number, clean, high altitude, considerably in excess of 2; maximum IAS achieved, in excess of 800kts (921mph, 1,483km/h) (possibly a record for any aircraft); achieved time from brakes-release to 30,000ft (9,150m), less than 2 minutes; mission radius, hi-lo-lo-high with weapon load, 864 miles (1,390km); ferry mission, 2,420 miles (3,892km); airfield performance, can operate from any 3,000ft (915m) strip, with take-off at 58,400lb (26.5 tonnes); approach at 115kts (215km/h) and landing run 1,200ft (370m).

Tornado Development Aircraft (01-09 prototypes, 10 static test, 11-16 pre-production)

No	Serial	First flight	Location	Front seat	Back seat	Remarks
01	D-9591	14 August 74	Manching	Paul Millett	Nils Meister	Serial later 98+04
02	XX946	30 October 74	Warton	Paul Millett	Pietro Trevisan	
03	XX947	5 August 75	Warton	David Eagles	Tim Ferguson	First dual-control
04	D-9592	2 September 75	Manching	Hans-Friedrich Rammensee	Nils Meister	Integrated avionic system, later 98+05
05	X-586	5 December 75	Caselle	Pietro Trevisan	test gear	
06	XX948	20 December 75	Warton	David Eagles	test gear	Gun fitted, slim rear fuselage
07	98+06	30 March 76	Manching	Nils Meister	Fritz Eckert	Almost complete avionics
08	XX949	15 July 76	Warton	Paul Millett	Ray Woolett	
09	X-587	5 February 77	Caselle	Pietro Trevisan	Manlio Quarantelli	
11	98+01	5 February 77	Manching	Hans-Friedrich Rammensee	Kurt Schreiber	Dual-control
12	XZ630	14 March 77	Warton	Tim Ferguson	Roy Kenward	
13	98+02	10 January 78	Manching	Fritz Soos	Rainer Henke	Kinked taileron
14	X-588	8 January 79	Caselle	Manlio Quarantelli	Egidio Nappi	Production wings
15	XZ631	24 November 78	Warton	Jerry Lee	Jim Evans	Production rear fuselage/wet fin
16	98+03	26 March 79	Manching	Armin Krauthann	Fritz Eckert	Production forward fuselage

111

Above: No other fighter comes anywhere near matching the very long range and great flight endurance of the F2 except for types that burn fuel at from $2\frac{1}{2}$ to 4 times the rate; in speed it also combines unsurpassed performance with economy, and the newest cockpit in the business./*BAe*

Below: Curiously, some people have 'knocked' the Tornado on the grounds that it is too big, instead of being a nimble modern combat platform. How wrong this view is can best be shown by simply looking at an IDS Tornado in company with other modern combat machines: an F-111E from Upper Heyford, an F-15 from Bitburg and an F-4F from Wittmundhafen./*Wegemann*